LETTERS OF THE HOLY PROPHET

Sultan Ahmed Qureshi

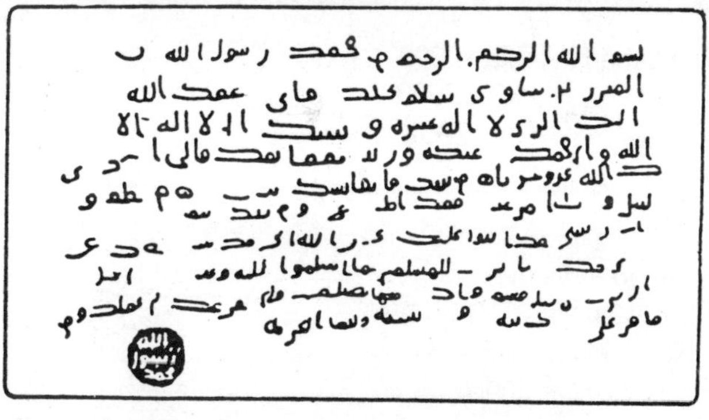

KITAB BHAVAN

New Delhi-110002 (India)

KITAB BHAVAN
Publishers, Distributors, Exporters & Importers
1784, Kalan Mahal, Darya Ganj
New Delhi-110002 (India)

Phone : (91-11) 23277392, 23277393, 23274686
Fax : (91-11) 23263383
E-mail : nasri@vsnl.com
Website: www.kitabbhavan.com

ISBN : 81-7151-296-8

Book Code No. L00009

First Published in India : 2000
Reprented : 2003
Reprinted : 2008

Published in India by:
Nusrat Ali Nasri for KITAB BHAVAN
1784, Kalan Mahal, Darya Ganj
New Delhi-110002 (India)

Printed in India at:
H.S. Printers
New Delhi-110002

CONTENTS

PART III – LETTERS & INJUNCTIONS SENT TO THE CHIEFTAINS, LEADERS & HEADS OF VARIOUS TRIBES & INDIVIDUALS

PART IV - THE INJUNCTIONS, ORDERS, INSTRUCTIONS, DEEDS, ETC., OF THE HOLY PROPHET (S.A.W.) SENT TO DIFFERENT HEADS OF TRIBES & INDIVIDUALS

List of the Photographs of the Sacred Letters of the Holy Prophet (S.A.W.)

Abbreviations Used

1. S.A.W. Sal-lal-laho 'Alaitul wa Sal-lam
   (Peace be upon him)

2. R.A.A. Radi Allaho 'Anhu – or 'Anha – or 'Anhum
   (Allah will be pleased with him – or her – or with them)

3. R.A. Rahmat-Allah-e-'Alaih
   (Allah's mercy be upon him)

بِسْمِ اللّٰهِ الرَّحْمٰنِ الرَّحِيْمِ

LETTERS OF THE HOLY PROPHET (S.A.W)

INTRODUCTION

This book is a compilation of the letters, treaties, agreements and injunctions of the most praised of all human beings. He was the foremost law-giver of the world. He gave real dignity, equality and justice to mankind. He showed the right and straight path to his fellow beings.

He is most praised, as there has been none on whom praise was showered continuously day and night, is being showered and shall continue to be showered for ever. There have been hundreds of thousands of prophets, heroes, leaders, conquerors, warriors and benefactors. Even the names of most of them are not known to us today, some live only in pages of history. Hundreds of books have been written about some of them. It is, however, an incontrovertible fact that the number of books written on the life of Holy Prophet Muhammad, Sal-lal-laho Alaihe Wasallam (may peace be on him), far exceed the number of books written on the life of any other men taken together. Of all men, only one personality stands out, unique and alone on whom, not a second passes, in which thousands and thousands of people around the world, do not invoke the blessings of Allah. Whenever a Muslim hears the name of the Holy Prophet (S.A.W.), he recites Salat (peace and blessings of Allah) on him. When the words "Rafa'na Laka Zikrak" (We have elevated your account. (Al-Quran, 94:4)) was revealed to the Holy Prophet (S.A.W.), the Quraish were subjecting the Muslims to most abject humiliation, oppression utmost tyranny and inhuman cruelty, in the hope that the Muslims would succumb to their barbaric pressure; none except the Muslims could believe that the Holy Prophet (S.A.W.) would be the most highly praised man in very near future. But only a few years later the Quraish themselves began to praise him most of all. This is not the view of the Muslims alone, but has been attested by a profound non-Muslim researcher of America, Ripley who in volume II of his famous book "Believe it or Not" has statistically disclosed that the voice which is heard throughout the world, with complete uniformity; is one sound and it is the voice of 'AZAN' (Call to Prayer). This, no doubt, is a unique and unparalleled phenomenon. In the Azan, the name of the Holpy Prophet (S.A.W.) is recited twice, five times daily in Takbeer (call to set up and start Prayers) and in the Prayers.

The Holy Prophet (S.A.W.) is admittedly the foremost law-giver of the world, as he gave it, its first written constitution. Before this, written laws and regulations were available, but written constitution as distinct from common laws, was not traceable anywhere. This was given in the shape of the Treaty of Madina, comprising 52 Clauses. It established a system entirely based on justice, equality and piety and not on racialism, colour or language. This is again borne out by the plaque at Lincoln's Inn, in which the name of the Holy Prophet (S.A.W.) appears at the top.

As regards, the right and straight course to be followed by the humanity at large, the Holy Prophet (S.A.W.), unequivocally pointed out that Serate Mustaqeem (Straight path) leading to Allah is obeying Allah: doing Ma'roof (what Allah Commands us to do) and abstaining from Munkar (what Allah wants us to avoid). He (S.A.W.) also admonished the Muslims always to tread the "middle course" and not to follow an extreme course of action. He, in clear and definite terms, indicated that the right path is one and only one and that is the path of Islam, to which the mankind was guided by all the Prophets(A.S.)

Before a brief idea of the teachings of Islam and lifework of the Holy Prophet (S.A.W.) is given, it seems appropriate, to present a concise survey of the conditions and atmosphere existing in Arabia in particular and in the world in general, at that time.

The Arabian Peninsula is situated at the junction of the continents of Asia, Africa and Europe. To its east is the Arabian Gulf and to the West Red Sea. In the north of Arabia are Jordan, Iraq and Syria, and in the South Indian Ocean. The area is about 20,72,000 Square Kilometers. The major part of the country is desert. Mountain ranges are strewn throughout the country - the longest range is Jabal-us-Serat, which runs from Yemen in the South to Syria in the north. Some parts of Arabia are very fertile and verdant, such as the valley of Yemen and the hills of Taif. The surface of Al-Hijr is rugged and rocky and the Central Arabia is desert and devoid of grass or water. There are Oasis around which date-palm gardens grow.

Arabia is rich in mineral oil, gold and silver mines. At present it is the biggest supplier of Oil.

When Islam came to Arabia there were mainly two tribes, who were the real dwellers of the land. One was Banu Ismail, the descendants of the Prophet Ismail (A.S.) and the other Abu Qahtan. The former is also called Adnani tribe. There were also small colonies of Jews, in different parts of the country. Thus the population of the Arabia at that time comprised these three elements. Small innumerable branches and sub-branches of these tribes were scattered throughout the country. In this book names of different tribes and subtribes, to whom the Holy Prophet (S.A.W.) sent letters and injunctions, will frequently appear. It would therefore, be helpful to refer to the brief genealogical chart given on the next page.

Although some parts of Arabia had attained quite a high degree of culture, it was mostly due to the influence of the neighbouring countries. However, conditions in the remote parts and places of the country remained primitive. The people in general, did not have even small conveniences. Similarly the creeds and beliefs of the people differed. Some believed in Allah, but the others did not. Mostly the people were idol worshippers. Although they did not consider idols as their gods, but they believed that the idols were means of approaching Allah. They, therefore, had a faith in the overlordship of Allah. Judaism, Christianity and some other religions also had followers. With the passage of time many fouled practices had mingled up with Islam, the religion of Ibraheem (A.S.). The result was that the religion taught by Ibraheem — the idol breaker, — was gradually turned into idol worship. This practice had gone to such an extreme that idols began to be worshipped in K'aba, the House of Allah. The belief in the life to come, punishment for sins and recompense for virtues was unknown to them, instead they developed an inflated sense of arrogance and false pride. Due to this, many people in Arabia buried their daughters alive as they considered that the girls would be a source of humiliation to them and would bring to them shame. Sacrifice of human beings was offered at the altars of idols. They did not know what incest was. It was permissible for a brother to marry his sister. Similarly two or more sisters could be married by a man at a time. Unlimited polygamy was common amongst the Arabs. Gambling and betting were their pastimes. Drinking, adultery and lechery were the order of the day. Lack of modesty and absence of shame had gone to such an extent that narratives of debauchery and rape were recited in public.

In wars, it was considered right to burn people alive, rip open the bellies of women and put to sword babies. The Arabs were well-known for their barbarity and perversity throughout the world. Small incidents were sufficient to provoke bloody feuds which lasted for years. Thus the Arabs, as a nation, had gone down to the lowest and meanest level of depravity and degeneration. The different tribes were constantly at logger-head with one another and fought amongst themselves. There was no unifying force which could keep them united together as a nation. Southern parts of Arabia were taken over by Ethiopia and the eastern portion was under the control of Fars of Iran, while northern areas were captured by Byzantine branch of the Roman Empire. Although the interior was nominally free, but the powerful neighbouring countries wanted to capture it.

Independence within the country had a very derogatory effect on the people and created in them a sense of vanity and self-conceit. They wanted to excel one another by suppressing their own country men. They employed their rich language for self-praise, to humiliate others or to publicise their own lewdness.

The moral atmosphere of the world, in general, was no better than that prevailing in Arabia, during the 5th and 6th Century. The old civilization and culture was gradually crumbling down and in its place decay, disorder and chaos was setting in. The codes of ethics, rules and regulations evolved after centuries of hard labour and trials, were being disregarded and ignored, and in their place dissipation and disintegration was creeping in. It was evident that a reign of disorder, disruption and brutality was seizing the entire universe. Jewish and Christian faiths had proved quite helpless to bring the people back to the path of justice peace, human dignity and morality. Erosion and corrosion of original religious practices, tenets and faith, brought about by the passage of time, factional fights, apathy, self-interest and loss of the original texts of the holy scriptures, deflected the people from the straight course. Extraneous matter was introduced into the text of the Scriptures. It was the result of this divergence that the Jews claimed that the Prophet Ozair (A.S.) was the son of God, as he wrote the entire Torait (Torah) out of his memory. So did the Christians, who split God into three; God Himself as Father, Isa (A.S.) son of God and the Holy Ghost, although the teaching of Islam has throughout been that Allah, the Almighty has no need of a son or an associate, as He is above these limitations. He is All Powerful and All Knowing. The Christians preached Christianity to the Arabs for about five centuries. The result, however, was that the number of converts was almost negligible. Similarly very few people accepted Jewish faith, although the Jewish Rabbis did their best to convert the Arabs to their points of view. These efforts were ineffective in stemming the tide of idolatry, sin, immorality, tyranny and perversity in the Arabian Peninsula.

Such was the extent of depravity, corruption and contemptibility of the society, which the Holy Prophet (S.A.W.) was sent to reform and bring it back to the straight and right path of Islam. It is not difficult to conceive the stupendous, arduous, hazardous and almost impossible mission which was entrusted to the human being who was born an orphan, who did not receive any schooling and did not learn reading and writing; who did not possess worldly riches; who did not have the support of any powerful authority and who did not wield any special influence over the people. He was only armed with his rare strength of character; unprecedented honesty and integrity and highest degree of truthfulness. What could be more miraculous than the fact that with the help of Allah and His guidance, the Holy Prophet transformed such a God-forsaken society into a God-fearing, devout, truthful and dauntless servants of Allah, within a short span of about two decades. None of the previous prophets (A.S.) was able to produce such a miracle. Prophet Nooh (A.S.) is stated to have preached throughout his life, spread over hundreds of years, but was able to gather around him a handful of followers who were poor labourers and artisans. There have been great leaders, reformers and heroes, but none could achieved such a spectacular success, despite the fact that in most of the movements, force, massacre, arson, destruction and other methods of coercion were resorted to. As a matter of fact, some of the so-called reformers openly professed that man-slaughter was a must in such movements. Islam stands firm against such killings, because Islam declares that there should be absolutely no coercion in so far as religion is concerned. That is why if someone embraces Islam, he has to declare openly that 'he accepts Islam of his own free will.' It has been estimated that the Islamic State which came into being, during the life time of the Holy Prophet (S.A.W.), expanded, on an average, of about 800 Square kilometers per day. When the Holy Prophet (S.A.W.) departed from this world, an area exceeding 2.5 million square Kilometers had come under his sway. During this process of Islamization hardly 150 men from the enemy side died. The number of Muslim martyrs amounted to about 120. World history cannot produce an example of such a revolution.

Despite this, some of the enemies of Islam have been making baseless allegation that Islam is spread by force, coercion and use of the sword. Nothing could be more spurious than this acrimonious assertion.

Not only did the Holy Prophet (S.A.W.) purge society of all its ills and evils; he knit it into a solid brotherhood and established a genuine and real welfare estate, in which all were equal. Some short-sighted people, often pestered the Holy Prophet (S.A.W) to produce miracles, so that they might be sure of his prophethood and he did produce miracles. It is not proposed to mention any of them here. To a judicious and unbiased person, there could be no greater miracle than elevating the most degraded and evil ridden people to such a pinnacle of nobility, and sublimity that they became a symbol of nobility and greatness for the entire world. There have been great and aggressive emperors and dictators, who had at their disposal, all the worldly resources, arms and men, to enforce their will. Some of them contrived their own religions or social systems and ordered the people to adopt them. Despite all their powers, paraphernalia and mechanisms of coercion, some of their subordinates reluctantly accepted their systems, but as soon as they died their teachings were also dead.

The present day dismal conditions do not seem to differ much from those existing in the 5th and 6th Centuries. Despite the fact that the world has made tremendous material advance but actually, it has been going down and down. Our development or progress could be compared to a seesaw board, whose end of scientific advance has been going up and the end of virtue, morality and nobility going down. It is true that machines of destruction have been so thoroughly perfected that the entire universe could be wiped out in no time. But has a sense of security, peace tranquility and trust been created? The more have we gone "advanced," the more problems of hazards, insecurity, distraction, dissipation, destruction, distrust, licentiousness, delinquency, degeneration, unemployment, etc. stare as in the face. The more are the countries advanced, the more they face these problems. The result is that peace of mind, contentment, patience, and feeling of security and safety are fast eluding man and in their place, schizophrenia, neurosis, melancholy discontent, despondency and intolerance are grabbing him. No amount of lotus eating could assist him in providing solace, he hankers after. There is only one and one way of relief from these tribulations in this world and salvation in the next and that is the way of Allah. It adequately provided a riddance from all these ills and troubles about 14 centuries back and can do so now.

It may, in this connection, be clarified that Islam is not a mere religion or a set of tenets for performing worship or saying prayers, as most people take it to be. It is in reality a Deen, that is, a way of life, which covers each and every sector of life. People confessing other religions make a definite distinction between religion and other sections of life. They very often assert, "What has religion to do with politics, business and trade". Islam, however, covers and concerns all walks of life whether it is commerce or industry purchase or sale, weighment or measurement, politics or social matters; justice or punishment; credit or loan; agriculture or land tenure; eating or drinking habits; personal hygiene or cleanliness; general behaviour or conduct; customs or practices; relationships or marriages; births or deaths — Islam provides complete guidance and advice in all such matters, whether they are trivial or important. it goes to the extent of guiding a man how to walk or talk; sit or sleep; eat or feed, behave with elders, particularly parents, or young ones, specially offspring; treat guests, passengers, beggars and the indigent. Then Islam does not merely preach high-sounding and impracticable morality, but it is a natural 'deen'. Whereas it lauds the man, who although in a position to revenge himself, but refrains from doing so. However, keeping in view the human nature, permits him to revenge himself, when outraged against; but only to the extent to which he is injured or wronged — an eye for an eye, a tooth for a tooth and so on. but high is the compensation with which Allah will reward him, if he forgives and forgets; Thus two courses are open: one for him who cannot control one's revengefulness and vindictiveness; and the other for him who is patient and contented and is inspired by higher and nobler values, instincts and considerations. But are there many who can gladly offer the other cheek, if slapped on one. The Holy Prophet (S.A.W.) himself demonstrated, what he practised and give an unparalleled example of his sublime behaviour at Taif, where he went to preach and was ridiculed by two chieftains, who, not content with their mean and despicable behaviour, sent after the Holy Prophet (S.A.W.) some ruffians and urchins who pelted stones and rocks at him to such an extent that his shoes were filled with blood. (A full account of this vile behaviour appears elsewhere in this book). But instead of invoking a curse on the callous miscreants, he prayed to Allah to guide them and to give them an insight to enable them to differentiate between good and evil. Only a short time later, when the same chieftains went to the Holy Prophet (S.A.W) to make a treaty of peace, he treated them with kindness and regard. A similar demonstration of the blessed behaviour was seen on the occasion of the victory of Mecca, where the Quraish had subjected him and his companions to merciless torture and misery. He generously forgave all the mischief mongers and gave a general amnesty to all of them. Can our so-called civilized and modernised world produce a single example of such a high conduct. The behaviour and conduct of the big and small powers during the last world wars are still fresh in the memory of the people and make us hang our heads in shame. Even today the lessons of justice, morality, fair play and tolerance being taught to their satellites and weaker nations, by most of the big powers, make us shudder with pain and agony. If they persist in their present short sighted policy of mutual destruction. The day is not far off when this good earth would be reduced to shambles and heaps of ashes.

Amongst the most essential pre-requisites of a peaceful life in this world, justice occupies the most prominent position. For this reason, Islam has laid very strict and rigid rules for the observance of justice. But the world, as a whole, is drifting towards lawlessness or the rule of the jungle. Imposing law courts, proudly depict balances symbolising dispensation of justice without fear or favour.But actually the incessant legal proceedings are an exercise in hair splitting and interpretation of complicated legal jargon, in which each side tries to mould intricate points of law to its own advantage. This involves an endless series of argumentation and counter argumentation, which often, instead of clarifying the case, enshrouds it in the cobwebs of doubt and uncertainty, which can easily transform innocence into guilt and offence into piety. Similarly in international affairs, justice has become a travesty. A powerful nation, under the excusc of assisting a weaker neighbour, flagrantly grabs her, with impunity, without any compunction or digs powerful talons into her body politic; thus has a stranglehold on her and justifies it too. But if any other power resorts to exactly the same 'police action' the former grabber raises hell against the brother grabber. Thus in our own time justice has acquired a new meaning. What is just for a big power, is not just for a small nation.

No amount of coaxing, threats, or propaganda could be of any avail, unless a full fledged and joint action is taken against such highhandedness. But why should any one thrust his arms into fire for another's sake. Islam, however, stands for complete and meaningful justice for everyone — high or low; master or slave and man or woman — all are equal in the eyes of Islam. The injunction of Islam is that no amount of enmity or hatred against anyone, should deter a person from treading the path of justice and righteousness.

Although it was against the spirit of justice and religion, the Jews had, somehow improvised the custom of killings the slaves of big masters and noblemen who were found guilty of murder. But the Holy Prophet (S.A.W.) emphatically condemned the mal practice and reiterated that all — whether big or small — were equal and whoever was guilty should be punished and none else should be made to suffer in his place. Islam strictly prohibits any favour to be shown to a near or dear one and giving of incorrect evidence, even if it goes against him. It goes to the extent of even forbidding equivocating or twisting of words, which might render an evidence doubtful. Similarly Islam provides guidance in other such essential matters.

The most important and distinctive feature of Islam is its universality. The other prophets who came before Islam, were mostly for particular countries, areas, cities or even villages. Similarly their teachings were for certain periods, tribes or generations. Although their teachings were, in general, the same, some of the religious practices and tenets were also confined to particular people and time. But Islam came to guide the entire mankind and for all times to come. No other prophet shall now come. It is, therefore, now the duty of all the Muslims, particularly the scholars of Islam, to take the message of Islam to all mankind and do all that is humanly possible to disseminate the message of Islam, so that no one may put forward the excuse that he did not receive the message, before Allah on the Day of Judgment. It is also incumbent on every man and woman to see for herself what is right and wrong. As stated earlier there is only one and one way which leads straight to Allah. Allah in his infinite mercy and compassion, has bestowed us with wisdom and faculty to distinguish between good and bad; evil and virtue. He has shown us the way and provided guidance; but He does not coerce us to follow the way He has indicated as right. It is for man himself to choose either the correct path or to follow the wrong road. On his own choice depends his salvation or punishment in the life to come. Let all men, whoever they may be, whatever country or nation they belong to, whatever language they speak, whatever their colour and to whatever strata of society they may belong to, come forward and think over this most important matter without prejudice, bigotry and predilection, with a sincere, just and clear mind. If one proceeds in this spirit of genuine exploration, Allah shall guide one to find the right course of action.

Obviously Allah did not send us to this world to grope in the dark. He sent His Prophets (A.H.) to provide guidance for us. The teachings of the last Prophet Muhammad (S.A.W) and his conduct and actions provide us with a beacon light, to put all our moral and temporal affair on an even keel. His blessed behaviour and example are before us. It is for us to study his noble precepts and to order our lives accordingly.

The entire life of the Holy Prophet (S.A.W) is like an open book before the world. No phase of his life, from birth to death, whether private or public, is hidden from the searching look of man-kind. Every minute of his life has so meticulously, accurately and scrupulously been preserved that no critic can detect any gap any where. Voluminous records, copious papers and traditions have been written and are being written about even the smallest details of his life. Never has so much been written in respect of any one else, however, great and important he might have been. Even the dates and time of most of the vents of his life are available. John Devonport in his book entitled 'Apology for Muhammad and Qur'an acknowledges this fact and testifies that it is an incotrovertible reality that of all the famous personalities of the world, nobody could be named whose life history is available with as complete and authentic details as that of the Holy Prophet Muhammad (S.A.W).

Just as Allah Himself arranged to preserve not only the original text of the Holy Quran, but each dot and dash thereof also; the life history of the Holy Prophet (S.A.W.) and his spoken words are safe in the annals of history. The reason is simple to understand, and it is that the Holy Quran is the last book revealed for the guidance of man, till the day of Resurrection and the Holy Prophet (S.A.W) the last prophet sent to this world to give a practical demonstration of the teachings of the Quran.

In order that the message of Islam should reach all the countries, nations, tribes and peoples, the Holy Prophet (S.A.W.) went to different parts and places of Arabia and to the contignous regions to preach Islam. He addressed letters to the Kings, rulers and Governors of the adjoining countries, Chieftains of a number of tribes and clans and leaders of different sections of the people, inviting them to give up evil ways and to embrace Islam. He also issued a number of injunctions and orders to various groups of society and entered into agreements and treaties with the Quraish, Jews and different tribes. Although these letters, treaties, injunctions and papers constitute as important a part of the life history and work of the Holy Prophet (S.A.W.), his teachings and other facts of his life; most of them, unfortunately, remained unnoticed and obscure for a long time. Efforts were made to trace them out and to bring this invaluable treasure to light. The western world is till not very familiar with these letters and papers.

An openminded study of the letters, etc., would reveal the unique type of the mental, ideological and idealistic revolution which was brought about; the matchless principles which were formulated to raise the moral and social standard of the humanity at large and the righteous path which was demarcated for civilization and culture. They also indicate the extent and limits within which human urges and demands could be met. This superb and exalted education and training was destined to transform the world's most ignorant, backward and uncultured nation to the most learned, cultured, pious, virtuous and humane society.

The letters and papers of the Holy Prophet (S.A.W.) are of four categories. The first are the treaties, agreements and pacts concluded with the different tribes, clans, Jews and Quraish. The Second are the letters written to emperors, kings, rulers, vicegerents, and Governors; the third are the letters and injunctions sent to the leaders of tribes, chieftains and heads of clans, and the fourth are the orders, injunctions, deeds issued to the heads of tribes, groups and individuals. These have been presented in four separate Sections.

It seems pertinent to explain, in this connection, that the treaties, agreements and pacts were entered into, not only to safeguard the Muslims from troubles and disputes, but in the interest of establishing an atmosphere of universal peace and tranquility, in which everybody is given complete freedom of thought, expression and taking independent decisions. This clearly demonstrates that the foremost objective of the Holy Prophet (S.A.W) was to establish peace and tranquility. No doubt he gave a grand exalted, noble and inspiring lesson to the world. The treaties and pacts are, in fact declaration of peace, freedom, equality and justice. Through them the Holy Prophet (S.A.W) gave the non-Muslim citizens their fundamental or basic rights. These have in reality, the status and standing of most elementary and firm basic political principles, from which laws and regulations for the non-Muslims were subsequently formulated. Another very important aspect which stems out from these treaties, is they give a good idea or an estimate of the esteemed conduct, behaviour, habits and thinking of the Holy Prophet (S.A.W) and Islamic way of worship, tenets, legal and constitutional problems and the novel civilization of Islam whose foundations were being laid at that time. These clearly indicate what international and universal brotherhood, amity and unity really is.

As stated earlier, the Holy Prophet (S.A.W.) was the first man to give the world a written constitution in the shape of the Treaty of Madina. It has been mentioned that the Holy Prophet (S.A.W.) migrated to Madina, which was thus far called 'Yasrib' in the 13th year of his prophethood, when the Quraish made, his stay and that of his followers, almost intolerable. Thereafter, Madina began to be called 'Madina-tun-Nabi' (City of the Prophet): and it assumed the form of a City State. The city was declared Haram (Heaven of Safety), where killing and looting is absolutely forbidden, like that of the Haram-e-K'aba.

At that time, besides the two tribes of Ansar known as 'Aus' and 'Khizraj' there lived a number of Jewish tribes in Madina. In the vicinity of the city, there lived three tribes of Jews known as Banu Qainqa,' Banu Nazeer and Banu Quraiza. They had built strongholds and fortresses there. Banu Quraiza always sided with 'Aus' in fights and Banu Nazeer helped Khizraj. The two tribes of the Ansar always remained at war with each other. The Jews who used to sell arms to both the tribes, desired that the Ansar should always remain disunited and weak. After the migration, a large number of people from amongst the Ansar of Madina accepted Islam. The Holy Prophet (S.A.W.) united them. Obviously the Jews did not like this. Besides, the Quraish of Mecca, with whom the Jews were on good terms, incited the latter to violence against the Muslims and they further stated that they were preparing to invade Madina. The Muslims, therefore, felt very insecure. Therefore, the first matter attended to by the Holy Prophet was to regularise the relationship between the Muslims and Jews. He, therefore, entered into a treaty with the Ansar and Jews and thus the Treaty of Madina came into existence.

In the present day world, the different countries and nations have forged before them formidable barriers of hatred, bigotry, false pride and enmity arising out of narrow minded nationalism. This is in reality the root-cause of most of the ills which are turning the present day world into a veritable hell. The defunct League of Nations and the present United Nations Organisation despite much fanfare of publicity and propaganda, and colossal expenditure, have been absolutely ineffective in uniting the different nations. The world has, therefore, much to learn from Islam which means peace and tranquility. Islam absolutely discards narrow-mindedness, arrogance, false pride, avarice, injustice, tyranny, oppression and self-aggrandisement. In the eyes of Allah respectable and dignified is he who fears Allah most. And fear of Allah means complete submission to the Will of Allah, which again means establishment of peace, justice human brotherhood and dignity, amity, equality, love for all and hatred for none. The holy letters, etc., were written in that spirit. They are therefore, redolent of sympathy, compassion and good-will for the addressees. The end in view was to save mankind from peril and ruin in this world and the next world. It is now upto mankind to accept the word of Allah and save themselves or to spell their own doom.

The Holy letters are written in a very simple, factual, realistic and forceful language, and are completely devoid of rhetoric, verbosity and superfluity. Yet they are impressive, convincing and are a heart to heart communication. The addressees were invited to give up what was wrong and to accept what was right — the way of Islam. The letters clearly manifest profound truthfulness, honesty, firmness and conviction and deeply impress the heart and soul. At the same time, they are to the point, brief and succinct. A miraculous quality of the letters is that even after a passage of thirteen centuries they still retain their freshness, brilliance and beauty, which cannot fail to appeal direct to the human mind. They are simple, yet forceful. The sentences are short and pithy. It seems as if a galaxy of glittering jewels has been infused in them. Few masterpieces of literature could equal the beauty, simplicity and brevity of these holy writings. They are thought provoking. The prominent features of the writings are:

(a)The letters, etc. invariably begin with *"Bismillah-hir-Rah-*

man-nir-Raheem". (In the name of Allah, the Compassionate, the Merciful).

(b)The letters then indicate that they were from "Muhammad (S.A.W.) Prophet of Allah".

(c)Thereafter, the name or names of the addressees, alongwith their Surnames appear.

(d)The letters open with a sentence either in praise of Allah or an invocation for His mercy.

(e)Then follows the subject matter of the letters in brief, tothe point, forceful and highly cultured sentences.

(f)At the end appears the seal with the word Allah at the top, and just below it is the word "Rasul" and beneath it comes the name of the Holy Prophet "Muhammad" (S.A.W.).

Of the letters, which the Holy Prophet (S.A.W.) wrote to the rulers of the neighbouring countries, five have thus for become available in original. These Holy epistles were addressed to the King of Ethiopia, Ruler of Egypt, Emperor of Iran and Governor of Bahrain. Photographs thereof have been reproduced at the appropriate places. Late Emperor Haile Salasi is reported to have shown the letter written to the King of Ethiopia to a Muslim delegation after taking it out of his treasury.* The letter is written on parchment thirteen inches long and nine inches wide. There are thirteen lines in it, written in brown ink. However, "Bismillah" and the seal are not clearly visible. It may be mentioned here that the text of the six

---

* The Political Life of the Holy Prophet (S.A.W.) compiled by Dr. Hameedullah (pp 169—182).

letters which have thus far been found is exactly the same as is given in the books of "Traditions". Even if there is any slight or verbal change of any word, the meaning remains unaltered.

It may not be out of place to point out that the traditions are of two kinds namely literal, or verbatim, i.e. the traditions in which the words are exactly the same as were spoken by the Holy Prophet (S.A.W.). The other kind is in which the ravis (narrators) relate the exact sense of the traditions in their own words. The conformity and identity of the texts of the Holy letters found from different sources, with the texts found in the Traditions, prove that the letters have reached us with exactly the original texts. The accuracy of the texts also bears a reliable testimony to the fact that the narrators of traditions were endowed with unparalleled memory. This is borne out by the texts of the letters and traditions which are the same word for word — as have been used in the books of the Traditions and biographies of the Holy Prophet (S.A.W.) during the last fourteen Centuries. Even if there is any minor difference of words, the meanings are the same. Besides proving the faultless faculty of the narrators of traditions to recollect and recapture the Holy words of the Prophet (S.A.W.), it also goes to testify the extreme vigilance and watchfulness exercised by them in relating the traditions. Even very long 'Ahadees' (traditions) were safe in their memory.

There is another important factor which ensured the veracity and absolutely correct communication of the traditions to posterity. The Muslims evolved and developed a highly scientific and rational technique of 'Asma-ur-Rijal' (Biography). The first principle of the technique is called 'Riwayat' according to which whatever account is 'given' should be stated by the person who himself saw it or participated in it. In case he himself was not an eye witness he should link the names of all the narrators *seriatim* upto the narrator who participated in the event. Then it should be assured what sort of people, the narrators were? What was their profession or hobby? Of what sort was their character and conduct? How strong was their memory? What was the level of their intelligence and power of understanding — whether profound or superficial? Whether pious, God-fearing and reliable? (*Seerat-un-Nabi* by Shibli Nomani, vol. 1,p. 37) Whether they were scholarly or illiterate? Whether they were well-known for their truthfulness or did they ever lie? It may be pointed out in this connection that the biography of the Holy Prophet (S.A.W.) began to be recorded approximately a hundred years after his prophethood. Therefore, the authors of his biographies had no authentic recorded material, but only verbal narrations; to help them. In such circumstances any other writer usually falls back on any material he is able to collect, most of which is hearsay or gossip, without caring from whom it originated. Subsequently such record takes the shape of history. Most of the historical writers of Europe were wont to adopt — this easy line.

The Muslims, however, proceeded with a great caution and discarded all unreliable material. They laid the foundation of true biography, which still remains unparalleled. As stated above, the first principle which they firmly followed was that of 'Riwayat'. In case they found any of the narrators unreliable, they rejected the reported material.

To ensure complete reliability, biographies of the narrators were meticulously prepared from very authentic, reliable and firm sources. Thanks to this technique, life sketches of hundreds of thousands of narrators are known to us. According to the learned Doctor Springer of Germany, accounts of five hundred thousand were recorded. The learned Doctor candidly admitted that there has not been any other people, who discovered such a technique, which could have made it possible to know the historical records of such a huge number of men. These records are not a mere collection of undependable data, but a result of thorough investigation. The character of each narrator was studied threadbare, without fear or favour.*

The second principle which was also firmly kept in view is known as "Dirayat," which means that whatever was related or narrated was in conformity with commonsense or in other words, if it was rational at all. If any event, occurrence or matter was considered to be against commonsense, reason, experience and not in conformity with the dictates of wisdom, or accepted practice it was rejected outright. This principle was also enunciated in Sura-Hujrat of the Holy Quran which states, "Oh! you who believe! if some mischief monger brings to you any tidings, you should thoroughly ascertain its truth, lest you should harm any tribe through your folly and thereafter you may have to regret your action". This was the basis of the compilation of the Traditions. However, high a narrator's position might have been, his words were subjected to closest and strictest scrutiny.

In the letters being presented in this book, there are frequent references to Iman, Salat, Saum, Zakat, Ushr, Khums, Hajj, Tauhid, Diyat, Fidya, Umra, Jiziya, Haram and Sadaqa and Khairat. It seems necessary to explain the meaning and implication of these terms briefly.

Iman: As regards the first five terms, it may be pointed out that these constitute the foundation of Islam. The first and foremost of these is Iman, which means a firm and unshakable belief in (1) Allah, (2) His Angels, (3) His Prophets (4) His Books and (5) Day of Judgment — the day on which virtues and good actions shall be

---

* Seerat-un-Nabi, vol. I, p. 37.

properly paid for and sins and evils duly punished. It is absolutely essential to believe in all these with a firm heart and to affirm it by word of mouth, as no good actions could take place without these beliefs.

Belief in Allah means that Allah is One and He is the Sole Creator and Master of this world. He is aware of what we do, whether openly, or secretly. We should, therefore, do what is right, not only overtly, but also covertly. This is possible if the belief is real and firm and is the solid basis of all that is good and virtuous.

Belief in Prophets (A.S.) is also inevitable as the guidance and commands of Allah are received through them. Besides they are a symbol of purity and piety, and through their good actions and virtuous behaviour, present a superb and sublime example of conduct.

As regards the Holy Books or scriptures these are meant to convey the commands and guidance of Allah in writing. This makes the belief in the Holy Books essential. In the absence of this, there are no other means of knowing the Prophets and the commands of Allah.

The last constituent of Iman is the belief in the Day of Judgment. The next world is the inevitable corollary to this world, which alone would have been devoid of any meaningful purpose. Had there been no recompense or punishment for actions in this life, there would not have been any incentive for good work or good behaviour. Human nature is such that if a man does something virtuous, he expects a return for it. Similarly if he performs an evil, he and his conscience fear a punishment in return. This fear or conscientiousness makes him realise his duty, to do what is right and to keep away from evil. It, thus, follows that without a belief in the

Day of Judgement, it is not feasible to put the work of the reformation and betterment of society on an even keel. Islam, therefore, places a great emphasis on this aspect of belief.

Salat: Salat or prayer in Islam differs from worship in other religions and has a peculiarity of its own. In 'Salat' the Almighty is praised and His help, guidance and kindness is solicited. 'Salat' is also an expression of complete humility and submission to Allah. A Muslim stands before his creator in all humbleness, bows before Him and finally prostrates before Him, in token of fullest submissiveness to Allah. Prayers have to be offered in congregation five times a day, at the proper time — before sun rise, in the after-noon, before sunset, after sunset and in the beginning of night.

Salat not only keeps alive in man's mind the idea that he is subservient to Allah, but puts his life on a regulated schedule; keeps him clean and tidy, creates a sense of responsibility in him and strengthens his morality.

Saum: Saum or fast is not peculiar to Islam only, but it has remained an essential part of other religions too. The ninth month of the Islamic calendar — Ramzan is the month of fasting. The duration of the fast is from before dawn till sunset. During the fast one has to observe complete abstinence from eating, drinking, sexual indulgence and all sinful and evil acts. Even petty quarrels and show of bad temper, peevishness and anger is prohibited during the course of the fast. The exercise begins with the first day of Ramzan and ends with the last day of the month. Fasts create in him strict sense of discipline, patience, contentment and purity. Besides creating in him a sense of obedience to Allah, they produce a realisation that Allah sees all his actions and this is what keeps him away from any transgression of the holy restrictions, even when he is alone and nobody is seeing him.

Zakat: Zakat or payment of poor-due is a very important component of Islam. After 'Iman,' it stands next to Salat in importance. In the Holy Quran, it is mentioned along with 'Salat'. The reason is that whereas 'Salat' is, the most important component of the 'Rights of Allah', Zakat constitutes an essential part of the 'Rights of Man'. The literal meaning of 'Zakat' is purity and growth, because it cleanses or purifies the heart and mind of the one who pays 'Zakat' and develops virtues in him. The main object of 'Zakat' is to help the needy and the indigent and to provide them with necessities of life. Zakat is thus the share of the poor in the wealth of the rich. It is, however, obligatory on the payer of Zakat that he should not do it for the purpose of a show and that he should not make the receiver of the Zakat feel as if he is putting the latter under his obligation.The rate of 'Zakat' in a year on accumulated wealth, ornaments and trade goods is two and a half percent. On irrigated land Khums (five per cent) and on non-irrigated land 'Usher' (ten per cent) of produce is payable as 'Zakat'.

Zakat can be paid to the poor or indigent, paupers, collectors of Zakat, moneyless passengers, debtors, persons or institutions propagating Islam or for benefitting common people, relief from slavery and bondage and to pay money to people as an incentive to accept Islam and stopping opposition to Islam.

The institution of Zakat lays stress on the fact that all that a man earns is not merely the result of his labour or talent, but is a gift of Allah Who through a number of ways and means helps man to earn what is destined for him. This leads to the conclusion that the wealth earned should be shared with others. The real purpose behind this is that wealth should not accumulate in the hands of a few, but should be shared by all. The Islamic welfare state at Madina, organized the work of the collection and distribution of

Zakat in such an excellent and efficient way that after sometime, the payers of Zakat were to be found on all sides, but it was difficult to find out the receivers of Zakat. Can any of the socialist or communist systems stand a comparison with it?

Hajj : Hajj literally means intention of pilgrimage of Ka'aba. Islam makes it obligatory on every adult of means, to perform Hajj once in his life-time. Any one who despite having means of performing Hajj, does not do so, belies by his action, that he is a Muslim. When Ibraheem and Ismail (A.H.) constructed Ka'ba with their own hands, about four and a half thousand years ago, they prayed to Allah to raise such a group from their descendant, as would be obedient to Allah. This meant that the work which was initiated by them, would be completed by some one from his children. The Holy Prophet who was the descendant of Ismail did this work.

An intending Hajee (Pilgrim) has to wrap himself in tow unsewn sheets of cloth, preferably white. Thus he presents himself to Allah in the garb of a medicant, devoid of any toilet or show and as his humble servant. On the 9th of Zilhaj, millions of Hajees collect at Arafat in this dress as Muslims to solicit the forgiveness of Allah. It is a unique demonstration of the brotherhood of Islam. The people of different nations take off their national dress and don only one type of dress and on their lips is the slogan of *Labbaik Allahumma Labbaik* (here I am, Oh Allah here I am) which they raise incessantly, as if in a state of ecstasy and self-abnegation. It is, in fact, a declaration that all the Muslims belong to a single and unbreakable bond of the nationality of Islam. It is the creation of the cosmopolitan spirit, which the world stands in need of most at present — the need for moulding a brotherhood free from all distinctions of caste, colour, language, and narrow-minded nationalism. Islam provides a complete answer to that crying need.

Tauheed: (Oneness of Allah). As stated above, the whole structure of Islam, its system of faith and 'Iman' is based on a firm belief in Oneness of Allah i.e. Tauheed, which means none except Allah is worthy of worship and that He is the source or creator of all that exists in the universe. This not a mere belief but a solid fact of life and has a far-reaching influence over the entire human life. As long as a man believes in many gods or super-natural powers, he feels as if he is hemmed in on all sides, by forces of evil, oppression, affliction and harm. He is afraid of them and tries to appease them, by bowing before them. Once he has acquired a firm faith in One Creator, he is rid of that fear and develops in him selfrespect.He begins to realise that all power is in the hands of Allah and none else. He then develops in him a spirit of submission and humility and gives up despondency, dejection and hopelessness. In Islam to lose all hope, is a sign of disbelief in Allah. A true believer is always patient, persevering, firm, and resolute and avoids flattery, hypocrisy,bribery, avarice, greed and conspiracy.

Diyat : (Ransom money). If some one commits a murder, he is put to death as a punishment. However, if the next of kin forgives the murderer and agrees to accept compensation or blood-money, the murder is made to pay a fixed amount of money, called Diyat. Diyat has also to be paid for the loss of any limbs as well. Different compensation has to be paid for different limbs.

Fidya : (Expiration). Fidya is the money paid to get free a slave or prisoner or a compensation for a sin, etc.

Umra : 'Umra', like 'Hajj' is a pilgrimage to Ka'aba, but is a little different from Hajj. In 'Umra' there is no stay in 'Mina' or 'Arafat' and no sacrifice has to be offered. Besides, whereas there is a fixed time for Hajj, there is no fixed time for Umra, which can be performed at any time. Hajj is obligatory but Umra is not.

Jiziya : Jiziya is a defence tax, which the non-Muslim citizens of a Muslim state have to pay for the exemption from defence service in an Islamic state, and to cover the cost of the protection of their life and property and maintenance of peace and tranquility. In Iran this tax which was called "Gizeet", was being collected since ancient times.

The opponents of Islam, who have been very particular not to allow any slightest opportunity to slip by to slander Islam, without rhyme or reason, have taken great pains to make capital out of Jiziya. Although there is hardly any need to put out a justification for it, some of the Muslim writers, particularly historians have tried to put up an apologia in defence of this very reasonable tax. The matter, however, calls for a clarification for those who are unbiased and those who desire to know the real and hard facts of the matter.

Non-Muslims usually raise the objection as to why non Muslims alone were forced to pay the tax. As will be seen from what follows, the objection is malicious and simply meant to poison people against Islam.

Who would deny the fact that it is the first and foremost duty of every government to protect the life and property of all the citizens and to maintain peace. To provide this protection, money is needed and it has to come from the people. In all the highly developed and advanced countries of the world, the people have to bear the burden of heavy taxes for the day to day expenses of administration.

Islam has imposed a number of taxes, and 'Zakat', which a Muslim has to pay. Zakat amounts to two and half percent per annum on accumulated wealth, ornaments and trade goods, as stated earlier, and must be paid. Neither can the payment of Zakat be waived, nor can its amount be reduced in any circumstances. Besides, a Muslim has to make Sadaqa and Khairat (Charity). Once a query was made from the Holy Prophet (S.A.W.) as to how much should be given out by way of charity and Allah through His Holy Messenger informed that the people should spend whatever is extra to their needs. A Muslim man of means must pay sadaqa-e-fitr on the occasion of the end of Ramazan on behalf of all of his children and wife. On Id-ul-Azha he has to offer sacrifice of a goat, etc., and has to distribute meat to indigent people, as well as his relatives. A Muslim has thus to pay a considerable amount of money by way of 'Zakat' and 'Sadaqat'. But a nonMuslim has to pay only a paltry sum by way of Jiziya. The highest amount which the richest non Muslim has to pay comes to about 48 dirhams annually. (Kitab al-Kharaj by Qazi Abu Yusuf, and chapter on Jiziya, Durre Mukhtar). But this amount had to be paid by the one who had at least ten thousand dirhams in his possession or less than half a percent. Dirham, it may be explained, was a small coin of silver which is equal to about a quarter rupee in Pak. currency or 2 US. cents. The entire amount of Jiziya payable by the richest non Muslim came to about one U.S. dollar. As against this petty sum, Zakat alone payable by an equally rich man amounts to five US dollars. Other 'Sadaqat' are in addition to it. Then again whereas the small sum mentioned above is the maximum Jiziya payable; the amount of Zakat increases with the increasing amount of wealth. Thus there is no maximum limit of Zakat. Also the aged, children, women, the poor, the crippled, men rendering military service and religious leaders are exempted from the payment of Jiziya. But there are no such exemptions in the case of Zakat. Every body possessing wealth must pay Zakat.

The facts mentioned above go to prove without an iota of

doubt that the payment of Jiziya did not at all involve any injustice, high handedness or any biotry, as has been made out by many Christian authors. Nothing could be farther from facts or justice. As a matter of fact a more lenient, righteous and tolerant treatment could hardly be expected from any other religion excepting Islam. One wonders how bias and bigotry can transform a really virtuous quality into an evil!

Haram: Haram is an area or place, in which every thing acquires a sacred status. The grass and tree of that place cannot be cut; birds and animals not preyed upon or killed and no blood shed there. All those who go there are treated as if they have been given refuge during their stay there, even if they are criminals.

Sadaqat & Khairat: These terms stand for charitv in general, which a Muslim is expected to perform, in the service of humanity, irrespective of any distinction of religion, caste or creed. There is a definite injunction in Islam, not to rebuke a beggar, however adamant he may be, but to ask for forgiveness, if one is unable to give any alms. Even polite and kind words come in the category of 'Sadaqa,' in the eyes of Allah.

It would be appropriate to point out that the Holy Prophet (S.A.W.) wrote the first letter to the King of Ethiopia from Mecca, at the time when the second batch of Muslims migrated to Ethiopia, due to unbearable and inhuman oppression of the Quraish. The period of letters can be divided into two. The first period of the letters is from 8th year after Prophethood and the second from the beginning of the Treaty of Hudabiayya.

In the letters to Jews and Christians, the Holy Prophet (S.A.W.) generally laid stress on Oneness of Allah and on the fact that no human being howsoever big, great or powerful, could ever be equal or partner of Allah and therefore, not worthy of being worshipped or related to Him in any way. He (S.A.W.) also impressed on them to give up all matters in which there was a difference of opinion and to agree on to the thing which was acceptable to them as well as to the Muslims. In the letters addressed to infidels or unbelievers the Holy Prophet (S.A.W.) emphasised that the idols were absolutely devoid of any power or action and that all power belonged to Allah.

A close study of the agreements and pacts would reveal that they were executed in a spirit of reconciliation, friendliness, goodwill, justice and honesty. The Quraish insisted on the inclusion of clauses which were apparently repugnant to the Muslims in the pact of Hudaibiyya. The Holy Prophet (S.A.W.) agreed to them, although his companions were not happy with the conclusion of the pact on terms which appeared to be derogatory to the Muslims, particularly clause 4, which laid down that if a Muslim fell into the hands of the Quraish, they would detain him, but if anyone from the side of the Quraish was captured by the Muslims, he would be returned to the Quraish. The companions, however, showed complete obedience to the Holy Prophet (S.A.W.) Here was a real test of the Holy Prophet (S.A.W.), who was a real seer and who could foresee what an ordinary man could not. His prescience could clearly perceive the future and he showed extreme prudence in accepting the terms of his opponents. He was the harbinger of peace and therefore chose the path of peace and not conflict. He had full confidence in his followers and could foresee that if any of them, was taken prisoners by the Quraish, he, by his high conduct and character, would exert benign influence on the unbelievers and this is what actually happened. In reality it was a grand victory for the Holy Prophet (S.A.W.) and Allah the Gracious called it "Clear or open victory" in the Holy Quran. The treaty was thus a source of considerable benefits and successes for Islam in the near future.

The biggest achievement of the treaty was that subsequently the Muslims and unbelievers came much closer and this resulted in an intimate association between the two. This developed into near relationship and exchange of ideas and views. It was but natural that they began to lean towards Islam and its high values. The logical consequence of all this was that within a short duration of two years, a large number of people got converted to Islam. It is stated in volume 2 of the History of Tabari (Episode of Hudaibiyya) that the number of people who accepted Islam during this period, far exceeded the number who became Muslims during the long period of the past 18 years.

It would also be noted that most of the Holy letters were extremely effective. The letter which was written to Khusro Perwez enraged the latter as he considered himself a demigod. The kingdom of Khusro Perwez was vast and his wealth unbound and splendour of his palace fabulous.He could hardly imagine if a common man, whom he considered as his subject could write his own name before the name of the emperor and could dare ask him to accept Islam. He got so furious that he tore up the letter and roared "How a slave of ours dare address to us a letter in this way. The Governor of Yemen should be ordered to get hold of him and send him to our court". The Messenger of the Holy Prophet (S.A.W.) was bold enough to address the emperor and his courtiers and to point out to them that there were bigger Kingdoms than their kingdom, which was a small piece of Allah's land and of which they were so proud. He also made it clear that a righteous call could not be suppressed by their humiliating conduct. He then left the court and on his return related the incident before the Holy Prophet (S.A.W.) who observed that (just as the letter was torn) the Kingdom of Kisra would get torn within a few years, the great Kingdom shattered in pieces. *(Tabari's History).*

As stated above, Khusro Perwez had ordered 'Bazan', Governor of Yemen to arrest the Holy Prophet (S.A.W.) and to present him at his court. Bazan deputed Baboya and Khar Khasra to Madina to execute the orders. The two appeared before the Holy Prophet (S.A.W.) and with due respect and stated that Emperor Khusro had sent for him. He further clarified that if the orders of the Emperor were not compiled with, the latter would destroy him (the Prophet) and his country. The messengers of Bazan were taken aback when they heard the Holy Prophet say, "Destiny has turned the tables on your King. Khusro has been murdered by his own son Sheroya. You take the news to your master. Also inform him that he would soon come to know that the Islamic State would extend to the Capital of the Kingdom of Kisra".

It so happened that Caesar defeated Khusro and the Byzantine forces reached close to the capital of Iran. At that time trouble broke out in the family of Khusro, who was taken prisoner by his son Sheroya. It is stated in Tabari's History that Sheroya murdered his father on the night of the 13th Jamadiul Awwal of 7th Hijri i.e. 628 A.D. The messengers of the Governor of Yemen were highly impressed by what they saw of the high character and conduct of the Holy Prophet (S.A.W.), his extremely simple way of living and that of his companions. On reaching Yemen, they related their impressions and the prediction of the Holy Prophet. Bazan, too, was highly influenced by these talks and he said, "By his talks, he does not seem to be a wordly King, but certainly a prophet of Allah. Still we should wait and ascertain the prophecy".

When Baboya and Khar Khasra returned to Yemen, Bazan received a message from Sheroya that Khusro had been murdered on account of his highly tyrannical acts. He also directed that the Arabian Prophet (S.A.W.) should not be interfered with. Ultimately Bazan was convinced of the truthfulness of the Holy

Prophet (S.A.W.) and he entered the fold of Islam, along with a large number of his people.

(Tabari's History, vol. 3, page 91).

Despite the fact that the Holy letter addressed to Khusro Perwez was torn by him, it is a miracle that it resisted obliteration for over thirteen hundred years. It seems when Khusro tore and threw it away, somebody, picked it up and gradually it found its way to the collection of a Christian family of Lebanon and was ultimately discovered by the former Foreign Minister of Lebanon, Henry Pharaoh. The researchers who minutely examined the letter confirmed that it was the genuine letter written by the Holy Prophet (S.A.W.) to Khusro Perwez.

Part 1

TREATIES, PACTS AND AGREEMENTS

1. THE TREATY OF MADINA

In the name of Allah, the Compassionate, the Merciful

1. This agreement of Allah's Prophet Muhammad (S.A.W.) shall apply to the migrants, Quraish, the citizens of Yasrib (Madina) who have accepted Islam and all such people who are in agreement with the above mentioned bodies and side with them in war.

2. Those who are a party to this agreement shall be treated as a body separate from all those who are not a party to this agreement.

3. The Quraish migrants are in themselves a party and as in the past; shall be responsible for the payment of blood-money on behalf fo their criminals and shall themselves get their prisoners freed, after the payment of ransom. All this process shall be in accordance with the principles of belief (Iman) and justice.

4. Bani Auf shall be responsible for their own tribe and shall jointly pay their blood-money in accordance with article 3 and shall themselves be responsible for getting their prisoners freed after paying ransom. All this work shall be completed in conformity with the principle of honesty and justice.

5. Bani Al Haris shall be responsible for their own tribe and shall jointly pay their blood-money in accordance with article 3 and shall themselves be responsible for getting their prisoners freed after paying ransom. All this work shall be completed in conformity with the principle of honesty and justice.

6. Bani Sa'ida shall be responsible for their own tribe and shall jointly pay their blood-money, in accordance with article 3 and shall themselves be responsible for getting their prisoners freed after paying ransom. All this work shall be completed in conformity with the principle of honesty and justice.

7. Bani Jusham shall be responsible for their own tribe and shall jointly pay their blood-money, in accordance with article 3 and shall themselves be responsible for getting their prisoners freed after paying ransom. All this work shall be completed in conformity with the principle of honesty and justice.

8. Bani An-Najjar shall be responsible for their own tribe and shall jointly pay their blood-money in accordance with article 3 and shall themselves be responsible for getting their prisoners freed after paying ransom. All this work shall be completed in conformity with the principle of honesty and justice.

9 Bani Amr shall be responsible for their own tribe and shall jointly pay their blood-money in accordance with article 3 and shall themselves be responsible for getting their prisoners freed after paying ransom. All this work shall be completed in conformity with the principle of honesty and justice.

10. Bani Al Wabiyyat shall be responsible for their own tribe and shall jointly pay their blood-money, in accordance with article 3 and shall themselves be responsible for getting their prisoners freed

after paying ransom. All this work shall be completed in conformity with the principle of honesty and justice.

11. Bani Al-Aus shall be responsible for their own tribe and shall jointly pay their blood-money in accordance with article 3 and shall themselves be responsible for getting their prisoners freed after paying ransom. All this work shall be completed in conformity with the principle of honesty and justice.

12. If from amongst the Muslims, an indigent person is guilty of an offence, in which blood-money becomes due or he is taken prisoner and is unable to pay ransom; it shall be incumbent on other Muslims to pay blood-money or ransom on his behalf and get him freed, in order that virtue and sympathy in the mutual relationship of the Muslims may be created.

13. No Muslim shall be hostile to the slave set free by another Muslim.

14. It shall be the duty of the Muslims to oppose openly every such person as created mischief and riot and troubles human beings or forcibly wants to grab something and resorts to oppression. All the Muslims shall remain mutually united in punishing such a person, even if he is the son of anyone of them.

15. No Muslim shall have the right of killing another Muslim in exchange of an infidel (who is at war) or assist a person who is at war with the Muslims.

16. The promise of Allah, responsibility and protection are all one and the same. This means that if a Muslim gives refuge to someone, it shall be incumbent on all Muslims to honour it; although the Muslim providing the refuge may be a plebeian. All

the Muslims are brethren amongst themselves, as compared to others.

17. It is incumbent on all the Muslims to help and extend sympathetic treatment to the Jews who have entered into an agreement with us. Neither an oppression of any type should be perpetrated on them nor should their enemy be helped against them.

18. The truce of all the Muslims shall be one: When there is a war in the way of Allah; none of the Muslims leaving aside other Muslims, shall enter into a peace treaty with an enemy, unless the treaty in one and the same for all the Muslims.

19. All the groups who participate in war along with us, shall be afforded an opportunity to rest by turns.

20. The provision of subsistence to the dependants of the Muslim who get martyred in the way of Allah, shall be the responsibility of all the Muslims.

21. No doubt all the God-fearing and devout Muslims are on the right path and are the followers of the best way of life.

22. Neither shall any non-Muslim who is a party to this agreement, provide refuge to the life and property of any Quraish nor shall assist any non-Muslim agai st a Muslim.

23. If someone murders a Muslim and there is a proof against him, the murderer shall be punished. But if the next of kin is prepared to accept blood-money, the murderer could be set free after the payment of blood-money. It shall be obligatory on all the Muslims to observe this injunction without any exception. Nothing other than the prescribed injunctions shall be acceptable.

24. For a Muslim, who after accepting the treaty, has agreed to abide by it and he believes in Allah and the Day of Judgment, it would neither be permissible to create a new thing or practice, nor would it be right for him to have dealings with such a person as does not respect this treaty. Whoever infringes this injunction, the curse and wrath of Allah shall descend on him on the Day of Judgement, and no excuse and request for forgiveness shall be accepted from him, in this respect.

25. When there arises a mutual difference about anything in this agreement, the matter shall be referred for a decision to Allah and Muhammad (S.A.W.).

26. After the treaty, it shall be obligatory on the Jews to render financial assistance to the Muslims when they are at war with an enemy.

27. The Jews of Bani Auf, who are a party to this agreement and are the supporters of the Muslims, shall adhere to their religion and the Muslims to theirs. Excepting religious matters , the Muslims and Jews shall be regarded as belonging to a single party. If anyone from amongst them commits an outrage or breaks a promise or is guilty of a crime, he shall deserve punishment for his crime.

28. The Jews of Bani An-Najjar, who are a party to this agreement and are the supporters of the Muslims, shall adhere to their religion and the Muslims to theirs. Excepting religious matters, the Muslims and the Jews shall be regarded as belonging to a single party. If anyone from amongst them commits an outrage or breaks a promise or is guilty of a crime, he shall deserve punishment for his crime.

29. The Jews of Bani Al-Haris, who are a party to this agreement

and are the supporters of the Muslims, shall adhere to their religion and the Muslims to theirs. Excepting religious matters, the Muslims and the Jews shall be regarded as belonging to a single party. If anyone from amongst them commits an outrage or a breaks promise or is guilty of a crime, he shall deserve punishment for his crime.

30. The Jews of Bani Sa'ida, who are a party to this agreement and are the supporters of the Muslims, shall adhere to their religion and the Muslims to theirs. Excepting religious matters, the Muslims and the Jews shall be regarded as belonging to a single party. If anyone from amongst them commit an outrage or breaks a promise or is guilty of a crime, he shall deserve punishment for his crime.

31. The Jews of Bani Hashm, who are a party to this agreement and are the supporters of the Muslims shall adhere to their religion and the Muslims to theirs. Excepting religious matters, the Muslims and Jews shall be regarded as belonging to a single party. if anyone from amongst them commit an outrage or breaks promise or is guilty of a crime, he shall deserve punishment for his crime.

32. The Jews of Bani Al-Aus who are a party to this agreement and are the supporters of the Muslims, shall adhere to their religion and the Muslims to theirs. Excepting religious matters, the Muslims and Jews shall be regarded as belonging to a single party. If anyone from amongst them commits an outrage or breaks promise or is guilty of a crime, he shall deserve punishment for his crime.

33. The Jews of Bani Sa'alaba, who are a party to this agreement and are the supporters of the Muslims, shall adhere to their religion and the Muslims to theirs. Excepting religious matters, the Muslims and Jews shall be regarded as belonging to a single party. If

anyone from amongst them commits an outrage or breaks a promise or is guilty of a crime, he shall deserve punishment for his crime.

34. The Jews of Bani Jafna, who are a party to this agreement and are the supporters of the Muslims, shall adhere to their religion and the Muslims to theirs. Excepting religious matters, the Muslims and the Jews shall be regarded as belonging to a single party. If anyone from amongst them commits an outrage or breaks promise or is guilty of a crime, he shall deserve punishment for his crime.

35. The Jews of Bani Al Shotaiba, who are a party to this agreement and are the supporters of the Muslims, shall adhere to their religion and the Muslims to theirs. Excepting religious matters, the Muslims and the Jews shall be regarded as belonging to a single party. If anyone from amongst them commits an outrage or breaks a promise or is guilty of a crime, he shall deserve punishment for his crime.

36. The subordinate branches of the above mentioned tribes shall have the same rights as are enjoyed by the original branches.

37. None of the treaty makers shall take any military action, without the permission of Muhammad (S.A.W.).

38. No hindrance shall be created in the requital or avenging of an injury or a blow. Whoever commits a breach of promise, shall deserve punishment for it and whoever abides most faithfully by this agreement, Allah will may help him.

39. If a third community wages war against the Muslims and Jews treaty makers, they will have to fight unitedly. They shall help

each other mutually and there shall be mutual goodwill and faithfulness. The Jews shall bear their expenses of war and the Muslim their expenses.

40. It is incumbent on the parties to the agreement to treat each other sincerely and to wish each other well. None shall subject the other to oppression and injustice and the oppressed shall be helped.

41. The Jews shall share the expenses along with the Muslims as long as they fight jointly.

42. The plain of Yasrab, which is surrounded by hills, shall be a *haram* (haven) for the treaty makers.

43. The same treatment shall be meted out to a refugee, to which a person giving the refuge, is entitled; he shall not be harmed. A refuge shall abide by this agreement and he shall not be permitted to break a promise.

44. Nobody shall be provided a refuge without the permission of the people of that place.

45. If there is any occurrence or difference of opinion amongst the treaty makers, which might result in a breach of peace, the matter shall be referred, for a decision, to Allah and Muhammad, the Prophet of Allah (S.A.W.). Allah shall be with him, who abides most by the treaty.

46. None shall provide protection to the Quraish of Mecca or any of their helpers.

47. If Yasrab (Madina) is invaded, the Muslims and the Jews both shall put up a joint defence.

48. If the Muslims make a peace treaty with some one, the Jews shall abide by it. And if the Jews make peace with somebody, it shall be obligatory on the Muslims to extend similar cooperation to the Jews. However, in the case of a religious war of a party, it shall not be the responsibility of the other party to cooperate in it.

49. In the case of an invasion of Madina, every party will have to defend the part which is in front of it.

50. The helpers of the Aus tribe shall have the same rights, as are enjoyed by the parties to this treaty, provided they too show their loyalty. Whoever adheres to this treaty most, Allah is his supporter and helper.

51. If anyone of the parties to this treaty, has to go out of Madina, on account of the exigency of war, it shall be entitled to peace and protection. And whoever stays in Madina, shall also be entitled to peace. Neither shall anybody be oppressed nor breach of promise shall be permissible for him. Whoever will respect this agreement with his heart and will abide by it, Allah and His Prophet (S.A.W.) are his protectors. *

2. PACT WITH THE TRIBE OF JUHAINA

In the name of Allah, the Compassionate, the Merciful

1. The life and property of the Juhaina tribe shall be safe.

2. Whoever commits an outrage on them or invades them, they

---

* *Ibne Hisham* Vol. 1, pp. 178-79. Ibn Kaseer, ***Al-Bidaya Wal nihaya,*** Vol. 3, p. 224-226, and ***Al-Wasaiq-ul-Siyasiya,*** pp. 1-7.

(Juhaina) shall be helped against him.

3. However, whatever trouble or war takes place amongst their kith and kin or if it concerns their religious affairs, help therein shall not be necessary.

4. The good and God-fearing people living near these people, shall be entitled to the same rights as are admissible to Juhaina.[1]

3. SECOND INJUNCTION OF THE HOLY PROPHET (S.A.W.) FOR JUHAINA

In the name of Allah the Compassionate, the Merciful

Whoever from the tribe of Juhaina accepts Islam, says prayers, pays the Zakat, remains subservient to Allah and his Prophet (S.A.W.) and keeps on paying Khums out of the gains of war and declares his acceptance of Islam and keeps aloof from the infidels; he is in the protection of Allah and His Prophet (S.A.W.).

As regards the pawned property; of the payable loans, only the amount of the principal shall be payable, after (the debtor's) conversion to Islam. Interests on the pawned amount shall stand cancelled. As Zakat on fruit — one tenth of the produce, shall be payable. Whoever joins these people shall have the same rights and the same terms shall apply to him..[2]

Allah's
Seal: Prophet
Muhammad

---

1. *Tabaqat Ibn S'ad.* Vol. 3, pp. 64-67.
2. *Tabaqat Ibn S'ad,* Vol. 3, pp. 24,25,27.

Note: When after sometime, most of the people of the tribe accepted Islam, the Holy Prophet (S.A.W.) issued an injunction to these people, mentioning their duties.

4. PACT OF BANU DHAMRA

In the name of Allah the Compassionate, the Merciful

This writing is from Allah's Prophet Muhammad (S.A.W.). for Bani Dhamra.

1. These people shall have the security of life and property.

2. These people shall be helped against whoever attacks them.

3. It shall be binding on these people always to help the Prophet (S.A.W.) and whenever the Prophet of Allah sends for their help, they shall give help, but assistance in religious wars shall not be essential.

4. As long as these people adhere to the pact, they shall be assisted.

5. Allah and His Prophet have a responsibility in this pact.[1]

Note: A number of such pacts were concluded with the tribes living close to Bani Dhamra. Details could be seen in the *Tabat Ibne S'ad* — vol, 3, p. 24. The following pact with Bani Zur'a and Bani Rab'a of Juhaina is of the similar nature.

---

1. *Tabaqat Ibne S'ad,* Vol. 3. p.27.

5. FOR BANI ZUR'A AND BANI RAB'A

1. The life and property of Bani Zur'a and Bani Rab'a shall have security and peace.

2. Bani Zur'a and Babi Rab'a shall be assisted against any person who invades them.

3. But there shall be no interference in their internal conflicts.

4. The pious and God-fearing people living in the vicinity of these tribes shall have the same rights to which the people of these tribes are entitled.[1]

6. PACT OF BANU GHIFAR

In the name of Allah the Compassionate, the Merciful.

1. Banu Ghifar shall be regarded as from amongst the Muslims. They shall have the same rights as that of the Muslims and Banu Ghifar shall be subject to the same injunctions, as are applicable to the Muslims.

2. Muhammad, the Prophet (S.A.W.) has entered into a pact to safeguard their life and property and the responsibility of Allah and His Prophet is for it.

3. They shall be helped against such an enemy as invades them outrageously.

---

1. *Ibid.* p.24.

4. It shall be incumbent on these people to give help, when it is called for by the Prophet of Allah (S.a.W.). But in religious wars each party shall remain impartial.

5. Whoever contravenes it, this pact shall not stand as an argument (or excuse) for him.

Note: Bani Ghifar Tribe sent a delegation to the Holy Prophet (S.A.W.) and offered to enter into a pact with him. The offer was accepted by the Holy Prophet (S.A.W.) who had a pact prepared. Before entering the fold of Islam, the people of the tribe were highway men and were professional dacoits who looted caravans and tribes. Abu Zar Ghifari (R.A.A.) the well-known companion of the Prophet (S.A.W.) belonged to this tribe.[1]

7. TREATY OF HODAIBIYA

In Thy Name O Allah[2]

1. This is the treaty in which Muhammad (S.A.W.) son of Abdullah has made a compromise with Sohail son of 'Umar'.

2. There shall be no mutual war for ten years.

3. During this period, every person belonging to the two parties shall be safe and secure and none shall raise a sword against the other.

---

1. Tabaqat Ibne S'ad, vol. 3, p. 27.

2. As usual the Holy Prophet (S.a.W.) had "*Bismilla-hir-Rahman-ir-Rahim* written at the top of the agreement, but due to the objection of Sohail, the representative of the Quraish, "*Bisme Kallahumma*" was written in its place, according to the custom of Arabia.

4. If any person from amongst the Quraish goes to Madina he shall be sent back, but if any Muslim goes to Mecca, he shall not be sent back.[1]

5. The tribes of Arabia would be free to enter into treaty from the side of either of the two parties.

6. The Muslims shall return this time and come back next year, but they shall not stay in Mecca for more than three days.

7. They shall not come back armed and shall bring with them swords only, but these shall not be kept out of scabbards and the scabbards kept in bags.[2]

8. PACT OF BANI GHADAYA AND BANI URAIZ

The following pact was made with the Jews of Bani Ghadaya

In the name of Allah, The Compassionate, the Merciful.

From Muhammad, Prophet of Allah —

To the Jews of Bani Ghadaya.

1.2. This treaty is an outstanding example of the Holy Prophet's extreme caution to fulfil promises. The treaty was in the process of being written, when Abu Jundal son of Sohail, who had accepted Islam, and as a punishment thereof, his father imprisoned him, escaped from the prison and appeared before the Holy Prophet (S.A.W.) in fetters and requested that he should be rescued from the tyranny of the Quraish. The companions were horrified to see his condition. But honouring the treaty the Holy Prophet (S.A.W.) sent him back to the Quraish.

2. Tabari's History, vol. 8.

1. Responsibility in respect of the Jews of Ghadaya is assumed.

2. Jiziya has been laid down for these people.

3. These people shall not rise against the Prophet in any way.

4. These people shall not be exiled from their homes.

5. Nothing shall render this pact void.[1]

Allah's
Seal: Prophet
Muhammad

9. PACT OF NAJRAN

In the name of Allah, the Compassionate, the Merciful.

This pact of Muhammad (S.A.W.), Prophet of Allah is for the people of Najran.

1. Although Prophet Muhammad (S.A.W.), had the power to take a share from their produce, gold, silver, weapons and slaves, he treated the people generously and leaving aside all these things, he fixed for them two thousand hullas[2] of the value of one Auqia each, annually — one thousand (to be supplied) in the month of Rajab and one thousand in the month of Safar.

---

1. Tabaqat Ibn S'ad, vol. 3, p. 27.
2. Hulla is a kind of Arabian dress, comprising two sheets, which can cover the entire body of a man.

2. Each Hulla shall be of the value of one Auqia and whichever is of more or less value, shall be accounted for accordingly.

3. If instead of Hullas, something like armours or horses or riding camels are given it shall be accepted in accordance with its evaluation.

4. It shall be obligatory on the people of Najran to arrange for the stay of my workers. But they will have to pay taxes within one month. They should not be made to stay for more than a month.

5. If due to a rebellion in Yemen we have to wage war, the people of Najran will have to lend 30 armours, 20 horses and 30 camels. If any of the animals are lost, the people of Najran shall be provided substitutes.

6. The lives of the people of Najran and its surrounding area, their religion, their land, property, cattle and those of them who are present or absent, their messengers and their places of worship are under the protection of Allah and guardianship of His Prophet. Their present state shall neither be interfered with, nor their rights meddled with, nor their idols deformed. No Usquf[1] (Bishop) Rahib or Waqa, shall be removed from his office. The intention being that no change in whatever state every one is, shall be made (status quo shall be maintained).

7. Neither the people shall be punished for any past crime or murder, nor shall they be compelled to do military service. Neither shall Ushr be imposed on them nor any army shall enter their area.

---

1. These were the religious ranks of the Najran people. These are equivalent of Bishop (Old Saxon biscop, Old High German biscop Recluse or Hermit.)

8. If any one of the people of Najran demands his rights, justice shall be done between the plaintiff and respondent. Neither oppression shall be allowed to be perpetrated on them, nor shall they be permitted to oppress any one.

9. Whoever from the people of Najran takes interest after the conclusion of the pact, shall be excluded from my assurance.

10. No one from the people of Najran shall be implicated in the crime of someone else.

11. Whatever has been written in this pact, Allah and Muhammad His Prophet (S.A.W.) are guarantors for it, unless there is an order from Allah, in this connection, and as long as the people of Najran remain faithful and adhere to the conditions which have been made for them, except that some one compels them to do otherwise.[1]

Allah's
Seal: Prophet
Muhammad

Note: Najran which was the biggest centre of Christianity in Arabia is a district of north Yemen. There was a very splendid Cathedral which the Christians regarded as their Kaaba. Large estate attached to the Cathedral was a source of big income. When the people of Najran received the letter of the Holy Prophet (S.A.W.), they sent a delegation to the Prophet (S.A.W.), which studied the conditions and had discussions. The Holy Prophet (S.A.W.), invited them to a Mubahila (Invocation of Allah's Curse on the party which is in the wrong) and asked them to pray to Allah along with their kith and kin, to send His Curse on the liars. The delegation did not accept the challenge lest they should be des-

---

1. Bulazari, Futuhul-Buldan, vol. 1, pp. 64, 65.

troyed and agreed to conclude a pact.

10. PACT OF SAQEEF (TAIF)

In the name of Allah, the compassionate, the Merciful.

1. This writing of Muhammad (S.A.W.) the Prophet of Allah is for Saqeef.

2. Whatever has been written in this deed, its responsibility is that of Allah Who is One and does not share His Powers with anybody, and of Prophet Muhammad (S.A.W.) son of Abdullah.

3. The valley of Saqeef has been declared as Haram. The cutting of the wild thorny trees thereof, hunting therein, oppression, theft and evil actions in it are all haram (strictly prohibited).

4. Saqeef has the greatest right to Wuj.[1] Neither army shall pass through the land of Taif, nor shall a Muslim go there and eject these people from there. These people may do whatever they like in Taif and its valley and construct whatever building they like.

5. The people of Taif shall be exempt from Ushr, Zakat and Military aid. There shall be no coercion, in so far as their life and property is concerned.

6. These people shall be regarded as a group of the Muslims. They can, therefore move amongst the Muslims without any restriction.

---

1. It was a Sandy valley in Prophet's (S.A.W.) time. It is surrounded by hills. The present day Taif is situated in the same valley.

7. If someone is taken prisoner from amongst the people of Taif, they shall have the right to settle the case.

8. Whatever debt of the people of Taif may be due for payment on a pawned article and whatever debt on a pawned article may be payable till after the Ukaz[1] season, should be paid by Ukaz.[2] Allah has no responsibility regarding interest.

9. In the books of the people of Taif whatever debts are due for receipt till the time of their acceptance of Islam, they shall be in their right to receive them.

10. If an article belonging to the people of Taif, held in trust, is destroyed by the trustee, it shall be caused to be returned to the owner.

11. The people of Saqeef, who are not present here shall have the same safeguards and rights as are admissible to those present here. Whatever property they have in Layya, shall be secure like wuj.

12. Similarly whoever is their partner in trade or their helper, shall have the same rights.

13. If someone commits a financial or physical excess or outrage on the people of Saqeef, all the Muslims shall help Saqeef against the offender.

14. Anybody whose entry into the area is not desired, shall not enter it.

---

1 & 2. Ukaz was a fair, held for 20 days between Taif and Nakhlab before Islam. It was a sort of national literary arena. It is a valley which is situated at a distance of six miles from Taif.

15. These people can construct places for buying and selling in front of their houses.

16. A ruler for Saqeef shall be appointed from amongst them. Accordingly, Bani Malik and Bani Akhlaf shall have their own Amirs.

17. The people of Saqeef who will irrigate the gardens of Quraish, shall have right to half of the produce.

18. No interest shall be charged on the pawned articles. If they are in a position to pay the amount of pawn, they should pay it. If they are not able to pay immediately, they should pay up to the Jamadi-ul-Oola of the next year. And one whose time is up and does not pay, he has no doubt turned it into an interest transaction.

19. If the people of Saqeef are in debt, the amount of principal only shall be paid to the creditor.

20. If they have amongst them a prisoner, whom his master sold away, the transaction shall be regular. If he was not sold, his ransom shall be 6 she-camels, which can be given in two instalments.

21. Only a person purchasing an article, shall have the right of its sale.[1]

Allah'
Seal: Prophet
Muhammad

Note: As in the present day, Taif was the summer resort of the wealthy Quraish. Being five thousand feet

---

1. Abu Ubaid, Kitab-ul-Amwal, pp. 19 & 92.

above sea level, its climate is cool and pleasant. In the past it was full of gardens and produced fruits and vegetables. The City of Taif, is now a big centre of trade and is a highly developed and modernised city.

Despite the fact that the Quraish knew that the Holy Prophet (S.A.W.) was extremely noble, truthful, honest, charitable and truth-worthy person, they treated him with contempt, malice and animosity, when he declared that he was Prophet of Allah. Day by day their attitude grew more and more hostile and bitter. When there was little hope of their listening to the voice of reason, the Holy Prophet (S.A.W.) went to Taif to preach Islam there. But unfortunately the people of Taif proved to be more callous, unreasonable and tyrannical.

In the city there lived wealthy and highly influential people. The Holy Prophet went to the three brothers named Abd ya lail, Mas'ood, and Habeeb, who belonged to the Omair tribe, which was the chief of all other tribes and invited them to accept Islam. What the three said was derogatory and humiliating to the extreme. One of them said, "If Allah has sent you as a Prophet, you are tearing the cover of Ka'ba". The second said, "Did not Allah get somebody else for prophethood except you?" The third said, "I cannot talk to you. If you are true, it would be discourteous to talk to you. If you are a liar, you do not deserve to be talked to."[1]

Not content with this insulting behaviour, they roused the street urchins and rogues of Taif, to jeer and make fun of the Holy Prophet (S.A.W.). The result was that the rascals stood in line on both sides of the way. When the Holy Prophet (S.A.W.) went that

---

1. Seeratun Nabi by Shibli Numani, vol. 1, P. 232.

way, they pelted stones and rocks on him, till his shoes were smeared with blood.[1] When due to blows and wounds, his strength gave way, he sat down; but the callous miscreants held him by the arms and made him stand up. When he would begin walking again they abuse him and claped their hands.[2] The Holy Prophet (S.A.W) at last took refuge in a vineyard.

The Prophets (A.S.) were generally subjected to such injuries and insults. Some of them prayed for Allah's curse. Prophet Nooh's (A.S.) curse resulted in the destruction of a big part of earth, by the Deluge. But the Holy Prophet (S.A.W.) was sent for the good and benefit of the world, he could not even think of such a curse. His companion on the journey,Zaid (R.A.A.) requested him to invoke the curse of Allah on such a bad lot of people, but the Holy Prophet got piqued and said,. "Never! I have been sent as a blessing for the world". Thereafter he prayed, "oh Allah! Give guidance to my people and give them a sense to differentiate between good and bad." But the moral and physical pain which he under-went can be easily gauged by the answer of the Holy Prophet to the query of Aisha (R.A.) as to which was the hardest day of his life. He (S.A.W.) referred to that day in Taif.

11. PACT OF AKBAR BIN ABDUL QAIS

In the name of Allah, the Compassionate, the Merciful

From Muhammad, Prophet of Allah —

To Akbar bin Abdul Qais

1. Seeratun Nabi by Shibli Numani, vol. 1, P. 232.
2. Full account of this could be seen in *History of Tabari and Ibn-e-Hisham.*

1. In the days of ignorance, those of them, who took part in mischiefs and riots and the sins they committed, Allah and His Prophet have no responsibility therein. But in future, it shall be obligatory on these people to fulfil their promise.

2. Neither shall the supply of their provisions and grains be interfered with, nor shall they be harassed at the time of the ripening of fruit.

3. They shall have the right to the use of the collected rain water.

4. 'Ula bin Al Hazarmi (R.A.A.) shall continue to supervise them on behalf of the Holy Prophet (S.A.W.). It is obligatory on the people of Bahrain to cooperate with him.

5. It shall be incumbent on the Muslim army to share with them the goods captured in religious wars and treat them fairly and justly. At the time of religious wars moderation and the middle course of action, should be kept in view.

6. The two parties shall not be entitled to an alteration in this pact. These people shall neither alter any pact, or depart from it.

7. Allah and His Prophet testify to this pact.[1]

Allah's
Seal: Prophet
Muhammad

---

1. Tabaqat Ibn S'ad, vol. 3, p. 33.

Note: A chieftain of Bahrain, named Akbar bin Qais went with a delegation of his clan to the Holy Prophet (S.A.W.) and stated that as their way was unsafe, they were not in a position to come to him easily. They, therefore, requested that they be taught religious matters with the help of which they could distinguish between right and wrong, so that they could take them to their clan. The Holy Prophet (S.A.W.) taught them about the Oneness of Allah, his prophethood, prayers, Zakat, fasts etc. He also gave them the above pact.

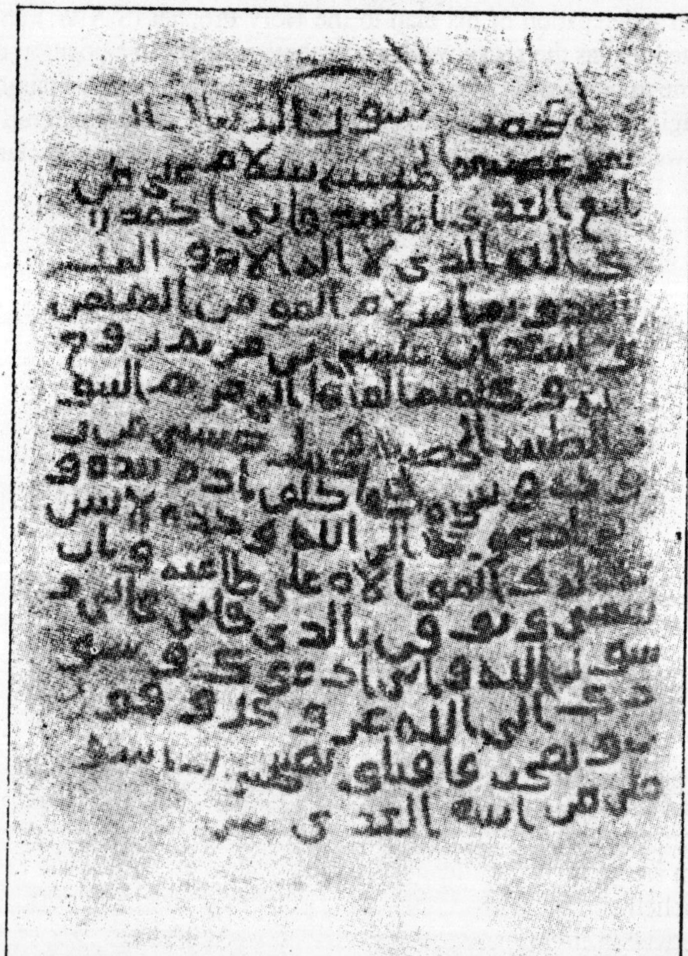

Letter of the Holy Prophet Muhammad (S.A.W.) sent to Negus, King of Ethiopia

PART II

LETTERS TO EMPERORS, KINGS, RULERS, VICEGERENTS, GOVERNORS, ETC.

1. LETTER TO NEGUS, KING OF ETHIOPIA

In the name of Allah, the Compassionate, the Merciful.

From Muhammad (S.A.W.) Prophet of Allah to Negus

King of Ethiopia.

I praise Allah, except Whom there is none to be worshipped, who is the Ruler of the world. He is innocent and pure (free from all blemishes, defects, flaws, or shortcomings). He gives refuge and sustains all.

I do admit that Isa (Jesus) (A.S.) son of Mariam (Mary), was the soul from Allah and His word (Order), he was infused to Mariam, who was clean and proof against evil. And Isa(A.S.) was born of Mariam. Allah created him from His soul and breath in the same manner as He created Adam(A.S.) with His own hand. I invite you towards Allah the One who has no associate. Believe in Him and join me in obedience to Him. Follow me and accept my prophethood because I am the Messenger of Allah. I have wished you well in conveying the message of Allah in all sincerity. It is up to you to accept my sympathetic advice. Extend the same invitation to your subjects. I am sending my cousin Jaffer (R.A.A.), with the other Muslims. When they reach you, treat them hospitably, by setting aside the vanity and pride of a ruler.

Peace be on him, who followed the right path.[1]

Note: As mentioned earlier, after the Holy Prophet began to preach Islam, the Quraish became the bitterest enemies of Islam. In the beginning they taunted, teased and maltreated the Muslims. But by and by their opposition took the shape of tyranny. Their treatment of the Muslims, particularly of the poorer ones was so brutal, that they felt extremely unsafe in Mecca and feared annihilation at the hands of the Quraish. At that stage, (6th year before Hijri i.e. 614 A.D.) the Holy Prophet (S.A.W.) allowed the Muslims to temporarily migrate to Ethiopia, as he expected a good treatment by the King of Ethiopia. The Muslims began to migrate to the neighbouring country of Ethiopia. This continued till the famous Migration of the Holy Prophet, after which the migrants began to return to Madina. The last caravan returned from Ethiopia in 7th Hijri - about 629 A.D. when the second Caravan went to Ethiopia, the Holy Prophet (S.A.W.) addressed a letter to the King of Ethiopia.

The Quraish could not tolerate that the Muslims should live in peace even in Ethiopia. They sent a delegation to Negus and pointed out to him that the Muslims had a strange faith which was altogether new and requested that the Muslims should be sent back. The King enquired from the Muslims about their beliefs. On that occasion Jaffer (R.A.) made a very impressive speech, saying.

"They were an extremely ignorant and pagan nation who worshipped selfmade idols. Debauchery, cruelty and eating the dead was their way of life, but Allah sent a Prophet (S.A.W.) who changed their lives altogether. He admonished them to worship Allah only and to regard Him as their Master. He preached to them

1. Tabari's History, vol. 3. 789.

always to be truthful; and not to misappropriate a trust, treat neighbours kindly, avoid bloodshed and all that Allah has prohibited. Worship Allah, the One observe fasts and pay Zakat. This was the crime, for which their countrymen forced them to leave their hearths and homes and they had to take refuge in Ethiopia."

The King of Ethiopia was highly moved by the speech and clearly announced that he would not allow such pious people to be tyrannised.

The Muslims, thereafter, always had a deep regard for Ethiopia and never did they think of attacking that country. They conquered big countries like Iran, but never touched the neighbouring Ethiopia.

2. LETTER TO ABU SUFYAN

Received your letter. I know that you have ever been steeped in pride and arrogance against Allah the Supreme.

You have mentioned of an attack to be made on Madina with a valiant army, which is bent on laying waste Madina. Let it be clear to you that this depends on the Will of Allah! If He will so wish, He could deprive you of the power even to utter the names of Lat[1] and Uzza.[2] You are amazed that I did not know the ditch method(for defence). You should know that this method has been made known to me by Allah because your wrath and rage has reached such a point that you are bent on dilapidating Madina.

You should know that far from your empty hopes being

---

1 & 2. Names of the two goddesses of Arabia.

realized, time has now come when Lat and Uzza, Manat and Naela[1] are shattered to pieces.[2]

Note: When the Muslims, due to the unbearable oppression, migrated to Madina, the Quraish started preparation to invade the City, so that the Muslims should not stay in peace. In the 2nd Hijri they invaded with one thousand strong army, whereas the Muslims numbered only 313. The combat took place at Badr. The Quraish incurred heavy losses and laid down arms. All their famous and brave leaders were killed. The second battle was fought at Uhud, in which the Muslims suffered heavily due to their not complying with the orders of the Holy Prophet (S.A.W). The combat was, however, indecisive. In the 5th Hijri, the quraish collected a huge army of 10 thousand, which included the Jews of Khyber also. This time they hoped to crush the Muslims in the very first attack. The Holy Prophet (S.A.W.) had trenches dug in the north of Madina and thus cut off the route of the Quraish. The latter were totally upset to see the trenches. Abu Sufyan, who was highly enraged, wrote a threatening letter to the Holy Prophet(S.A.W.) , in which he said that his big army would totally devastate Madina. The above letter of the Holy Prophet(S.A.W.) was in reply thereto.

The Quraish besieged Madina for several weeks, but could not capture it. One day a strong and violent wind blew which uprooted the tents of the Qúriahs. Their camels and horses ran away, and their cauldrons upturned. The result was that the Quraish were highly depressed and their courage gave way. The lost hope of a victory and left the battle field during the night. This was the last attack of the Qurasih on Madina.

---

1. Names of Arabic goddesses.
2. Dr. Hameedullah, Alwasaiq-ul-Siyasiya, Cairo 1941, p. 10.

3. SECOND LETTER TO THE KING OF ETHIOPIA

In the name of Allah, the Compassionate, the Merciful

From Muhammad (S.A.W.) the Prophet of Allah to Negus, King of Ethiopia. Peace be on him who follows the guidance. I praise Allah Who alone is to be worshipped. He is the Master of the entire universe. He is Sublime. Only He is the haven of peace and security. I testify that Isa (Jesus)son of Mariam (Mary) is the spirit of Allah and His word, which He communed to Mariam (Mary) the pious and thus she became the mother of Allah's Prophet Isa(A.S.) . Thus Allah created him from His spirit and infused it into Mariam just as He made Adam (A.S.) with His powerful hand.

Now I invite you to accept the obedience, sympathy, and love of Allah Who is One and Who is without an associate. You should follow me and should believe in the message of Allah which I have brought.

I call you and your army towards Allah Who is worthy of all respect and esteem. I have thus discharged my duty of conveying His message and advice. You should accept it, May peace be on the followers of the guidance.[1]

Allah's
Seal: Prophet
Muhammad

Note: As Negus continued to listen to the holy message, he

1. Tabaqat Ibn Sa'ad, vol. 3,p.15.

was being influenced by it. As soon as the holy text was over, he kissed the letter with extreme fondness and placed it over his head. He sent the following reply:

3.a. To Muhammad, Prophet of Allah. May peace be on him.

From As'hama, the Negus.

May peace be on you O Prophet of Allah! May blessings and favours of Allah be on you. Allah, except Whom there is none worthy of worship, Who has shown me the way of Islam and has guided me.

O Prophet of Allah! I had the honour of seeing your esteemed letter. Whatever you have written about Isa Jesus (A.S.) I swear by the Allah, Lord of earth and Heaven, that Isa (A.S.) is nothing more than that. I have well understood all these things which you have conveyed to me. Your cousin and his companions are my close companions.

I bear evidence that you are a true Prophet of Allah. I have taken bai'at (oath of allegiance to Allah and His Prophet) at the hand of your cousin, for the sake of Allah and have become a slave of Islam. O Allah's Prophet! I send my son Arha to you. If you will so order, I will present myself to you. May peace and blessings of Allah be on you.[1]

---

1. *Tabari's History*, vol. 3, p.89

4. THIRD LETTER TO THE KING OF ETHIOPIA

In the name of Allah, the Compassionate, the Merciful

May peace be on you. You treated us nicely. We have complete trust in you. The thing, we had hoped from you, has been realised and are safe and sound from the thing, we had feared. There is no capability (to do a thing) except from Allah. [1]

Allah's
Seal : Prophet
Muhammad

Note: The main object in sending the letter was to call back the refugees to Madina. The Negus is stated to have kept the holy letters in an ivory casket and said that as long as the holy letters were there, the people of Ethiopia should be safe and secure.

5. LETTER TO HERACLES CAESAR

In the name of Allah, the Compassionate and Merciful

From Muhammad, who is the servant of Allah and His Prophet to Heracles Caesar.

Peace be on him, who follows the right path.

After this, I invite you to the fold of Islam. Therefore, if you desire security, accept Islam. If you accept Islam, Allah shall reward you doubly and if you refuse to do so, the responsibility for the transgression of the entire nation, shall be yours.

---

1. *Tabaqat Ibn-e-S'ad*, vol. 3, p. 16.

O people of the Book! Leaving aside all matters of differences and disputes, agree on a thing, which is equally incontrovertible both as you and we are concerned and it is that we should not worship any one else with Him, nor regard any one else except Allah as our Sustainer.

If you deny this, you must know that we believe in Oneness of Allah, in all circumstances.[1]

Allah's
Seal: Prophet
Muhammad

Note: Just as in our time, there are two most powerful States which call themselves 'Super' powers; in the time of the Holy Prophet (S.A.W.) there were two most powerful States: One was Iran and the other Rome or Byzantium or Constantinople. The former was the biggest state of Asia and a cradle of a great civilization. It was towards the east of Arabia. Towards the north west was the Roman Empire. The two States were contiguous. Rome is at present the Capital of Italy. The Arabs called Byzantium by the name of Rome.

Some years back when this letter was sent, the Iranians attacked Syria and defeated the Romans. There is a reference to it in the Quran. The Romans, in order to avenge themselves, made big preparations and defeated the Iranians. Although the Iranians were at that time very powerful and the Romans did seem to have a chance of a victory against them, the Quran prophesied a clear triumph for the Romans. Heracles came to Jerusalem in token of his gratefulness, It was here that he received the letter of the Holy Prophet (S.A.W.). He ordered that somebody from Arabia, should be presented before him. Per chance Abu Sufyan was staying at Ghaza with his merchandise. The men of Caesar brought him from

1. *Sahih Bukhari*, vol. 1, P.5, Delhi, Asahul Matabe.

Ghaza.

Caesar held a grand court. He donned a Crown and sat on his throne. Then addressing the Arabs, he enquired as to who was the relative of the person who claimed himself to be a Prophet. Abu Sufyan said that he was related to the Holy Prophet (S.A.W.). The following dialogue then took place:

Caesar: To what sort of family does the Claimant to Prophethood belong?

Abu Sufyan: Is noble.

Caesar: Did some one else in the family claim Prophethood?

Abu Sufyan: No.

Caesar: Did someone from the family happen to be a King?

Abu Sufyan: No.

Caesar: Are the people who have accepted this religion, poor or influential?

Abu Sufyan: They are poor people.

Caesar: Are his followers growing in number or decreasing?

Abu Sufyan: They are growing.

Caesar: Have you ever experienced an untruthfulness from him?

Abu Sufyan: No.

Caesar: Does he ever break a promise or agreement?

Abu Sufyan: Thus far he has never done it. But it is to be seen if he adheres to the new peace pact which has been concluded.

Caesar: Have you ever fought a battle against him?

Abu Sufyan: Yes.

Caesar: What was the result of the battle?

Abu Sufyan: Sometime we were victorious and sometime he was successful.

Caesar: What does he teach?

Abu Sufyan: He says, "Worship One God — Allah. Associate none else with Allah. Say prayers. Take to piety. Speak the truth. Treat relatives with kindness.

After this dialogue Caesar remarked that the Prophets always belonged to noble families. Further he said that as nobody else from the family of the Holy Prophet (S.A.W.) laid claim to Prophethood, it was, therefore, clear that there was no hereditary influence involved in his claim to Prophethood. Similarly absence of any king in the family, proved that the Holy Prophet was not prompted by a desire of kingship. As He never spoke a lie, he could hardly be expected to lie about Allah. Caesar further observed that the followers of the Prophets, in the beginning, are poor and that a true religion goes on making progress. Also Prophets never cheat anybody. As he preached piety, cleanliness and worship of Allah alone, he should one day be a master of the place, he (Caesar) was occupying. Thereafter Caesar ordered that the letter of Holy Prophet (S.A.W.) be read.

The dialogue of Caesar, with Abu Sufyan, highly enraged the courtiers. The Caesar, therefore, sent away the Arabs from the court. The love of crown and throne and the opposition of the courtiers, however, did not allow Caesar to accept Islam. But his searching questions and his talk clearly show that he was convinced of the truthfulness of Islam, as he had correctly judged that a person who never in his life, uttered even a trifling lie, could hardly say anything wrong about Allah. He was also certain that worldly riches, splendour and ascendancy were not the aims and objects of the Holy Prophet (S.A.W), but the communication of he message of Islam to the entire world, was his mission.

When Caesar was about to return to Constantinople, he again advised his courtiers to follow the Holy Prophet (S.A.W.) as he was the one , they were awaiting. He further mentioned that their books contained the description of the Holy Prophet, Muhammad (S.A.W.), and these clearly and unequivocally indicate that he was

Letter of the Holy Prophet Muhammad (S.A.W.) sent to Khusro Perwez, Emperor (Kisra) of Iran

the true Prophet of Allah. It was, therefore, in their own interest to follow the guidance given by the Holy Prophet (S.A.W.).

The courtiers, however, said that it would mean their acceptance of the overlordship of the Arabs, although their's was the biggest kingdom of the world and their nation the greatest nation of the world. Caesar, thereon, said that although they were not prepared to accept Islam then very shortly they would be overpowered by the Arabs. He was much displeased by the arrogant attitude of the courtiers and immediately left Syria. While departing he looked at the Syrian territory and said that he was leaving Syria for ever. And it was true, he was never to return to Syria.[1]

6. LETTER TO KHUSRO PERWEZ, EMPEROR OF FARS

In the name of Allah, the Compassionate, the Merciful.

From Muhammad, Prophet of Allah to Kisra, King of Fars

May peace be on him who follows the guidance, believes in Allah and his Prophet. I testify that there is none worthy of worship except Allah, who is alone and without an associate and Muhammad is His Servant and Prophet. Allah has made me a Prophet and sent me for the entire world, in order that I may infuse the fear of Allah in every living person. Accept Islam and be secure. If you refuse, the sins of all the Zoroastrians shall be your responsibility.[2]

---

1. *Sahih Bukhari,* vol.1 p.5, Printed Delhi
2. *Tabari's History,* vol.3, p. 90 and Saheeh Bukhari

Allah's
Seal: Prophet
Muhammad

Note: The shock which his false pride received and his rage at being thus addressed have been mentioned in some detail elsewhere.

7. LETTER TO HURMUZ

In the name of Allah, the Compassionate, the Merciful.

From Muhammad, Prophet of Allah, to Hurmuz

I invite you towards Islam. Accept Islam in order that you may get security in this world and the next.[1]

Allah's
Seal: Prophet
Muhammad

Note: The Holy Prophet (S.A.W.) while addressing a letter to Khusro Perwez, had also sent a letter to Hurmuz, who belonged to the Iranian royal family and was the maternal uncle of Sheroya. Although at that time he did not pay heed to the Holy letter, subsequently he embraced Islam.

8. LETTER TO THE VICEGERENT OF EGYPT

In the name of Allah, the Compassionate, the Merciful.

---

1. *Risalate Nabaviyya*, vol. II, p.313.

From Muhammad Servant of Allah and His Prophet

To Muqawqis, Vicegerent of Egypt

Peace be on him who has taken the right course. Thereafter, I invite you to accept Islam. Therefore, if you want security, accept Islam. If you accept Islam, Allah, the Sublime, shall reward you doubly. But if you refuse to do so, responsibility for the transgression of the entire nation shall be yours.

O people of the Book! leaving aside all matters of difference and dispute, agree on a matter which is equally consistent between you and us and it is that we should not worship anyone except Allah and that we should neither associate anyone with Him, nor make anyone else as our god.

If you refuse it, you must know that we, in all circumstances, believe in Oneness of Allah.[1]

Allah's
Seal: Prophet
Muhammad

Note: Muqawqis who was appointed as vicegerent of Egypt by the Roman Empire. He was a great scholar of his religion. Egypt had always been a great centre of civilization and made great advances in various branches of art and astrology. It was also a commercial link between East and West. But like Iran, Egypt had also become

1. *Zadul Ma'ad*, vol.3, p.61.

Letter of the Holy Prophet Muhammad (S.A.W.) sent to Muqawqis, Vicegerent of Egypt

morally depraved.

Muqawqis was highly affected by the sincerity of the letter and he remarked that it was the time that the awaited Prophet appeared, but that he was under the impression that he would be born in Syria. He further observed that from Torah and Bible, he had come to know that the Prophet would not eat of charity, but would accept presents and that the poor and indigent would be his companions. He ordered that the Holy letter should be placed in an ivory casket which should be preserved safely in the government treasury. He sent the following reply to the Holy Prophet (S.A. W.).

8(a) TO MUHAMMAD SON OF ABDULLAH

From Muqawqis

"I read your letter and understood what you have written. I know that the coming of a Prophet is still due. But I thought, he would be born in Syria — I have treated your messenger with respect and honour. I am sending two maids for you as presents. These maids belong to a very respectable family amongst us. In addition I send for you clothes and a duldul (steed) for riding. May Allah bestow security on you.[1]"

Note: Just as Caesar could not benefit from the light of Islam; power and lust pulled him back from availing himself of the blessings of Islam. The gifts sent by Muqawqis were accepted by the Holy Prophet (S.A.W.).

The letter which was placed in an ivory casket by Muqawqis,

---

1. *Tabaqat Ibn S'ad*, vol. 3, p. 17

The letter which was placed in an ivory casket by Muqawqis, found its way into the Christian monastry of Akheem in Egypt. There a recluse pasted it on his Bible. The letter was written on a parchment. From there a French orientalist obtained it and sold it to Sultan Abdul Majeed Khan of Turkey, for a consideration of 300 Pounds. The Sultan had the Holy letter fixed in a golden frame and had it preserved in the treasury of the royal palace, along with other sacred relics.

High Muslim scholars have affirmed that the Holy letter was written by as high and sacred a personality as Abu Bakr Siddiq (R.A.A.).

Muqawqis, like Caesar, too had a dialogue with Mugheera bin Sh'oba, an exalted companion of the Holy Prophet (S.A.W.). Mugheera (R.A.A.) said: "Once I went to the court of Muqawqis, who enquired of me, about the family of the Holy Prophet (S.A.W.). I informed him that he belonged to a high and noble family. Muqawqis remarked that Prophets always belong to noble families. Then he asked if I had an experience of the truthfulness of the Prophet (S.A.W.). I told that he always spoke the truth. Therefore, in spite of our opposition to him, we call him *Ameen* (truthworthy). Muqawqis observed that a man who did not speak lies to men, how could he speak a lie about Allah? Then he enquired what sort of people were his followers and what did the Jews think of him. I replied that his followers were mostly poor, but the Jews were his bitter enemies. Muqawqis stated that the followers of the Prophets in the beginning are usually poor, and that he must be a Prophet of Allah. He further stated that the Jews opposed him out of envy and jealousy, otherwise they must have been certain of his truthfulness and that they too awaited a Prophet. The Messiah (A.S.) also preached that following and submitting to the Holy Prophet (S.A.W.) was essential and that whatever qualities of his had been mentioned, the same were the qualitíes of the earlier Prophets.

Mugheera (R.A.A.) was highly impressed by the dialogue. On his return from Egypt, he happened to meet a great Christian scholar, from whom he enquired if he awaited a Prophet, and if so, what qualities of his were mentioned in Torah and Bible? The Christian scholar informed him in detail that indeed they awaited a Prophet, and he would be the last Prophet. Messiah (A.S.) preached to them that when that Prophet appeared, they would follow him. He further preached that the Prophet would be illiterate and an Arab and his name would be Ahmad and his features and characteristics would be as follows:

"Middling height; big eyes with red capillaries showing in them, his complexion would be red and white. He would use coarse clothes and eat ordinary food. He would not be afraid of the greatest power; whoever would fight against him, he would face him. His companions would be prepared to sacrifice their lives at his slightest indication, and would regard him dearer than their own offsprings, mothers, fathers and brothers. From one harem he would stay in another Harem whose land would be rocky and where date-palms would be growing in abundance. His faith would be that of Ibrahim (A.S.)! He shall not adopt the way of the arrogant. His Prophethood shall be for all. The entire earth shall be his prayer - Carpet".[1]

Mugheera was so moved by talks that he went to the Holy Prophet (S.A.W.) and accepted Islam.[2]

---

1 & 2. Seoti, Hasan-ul-Muhazira, pp. 50-51.

9. LETTER TO HAUZA BIN ALI, GOVERNOR OF YAMAMA

In the name of Allah, the Compassionate, the Merciful

From Muhammad, Prophet of Allah —

To Hauza bin Ali

May peace be on him who follows the guidance. It may be clarified that my deen (faith) shall reach the boundaries of the entire Arabia and Iran and shall prevail. Therefore you should accept Islam. There in lies security.

I have nothing to do with your country. It shall, as before, remain under your jurisdiction.[1]

Allah's
Seal: Prophet
Muhammad

9(a) REPLY OF THE GOVERNOR OF YAMAMA

"The deen (faith) towards which you invite me, is very good. I am a famous orator and poet. Therefore the Arabs highly respect me. If you include me in your government, I am prepared to follow you".[2]

---

1. *Mawahibe Luddunniya, quoted by Risalat-e-Nabaviya,* p.314.
2. *Tabaqat-e-Ibn S'ad, vol. 3, p. 18.*

Note: The Holy Prophet did not accept the demand of Hauza. He usually refused such peremptory demands and would say that the matter was in the control of Allah, who gave His land to whoever he wanted.

A Christian scholar had advised Hauza to accept Islam and told him that the Arab Prophet (S.A.W.) would not have deprived him of his lands. He had informed him that Isa (Jesus, A.S.) had given the good news in the Bible, that a Prophet would come. Hauza, however, could not overcome the fear of losing his country and did not accept Islam.

10. LETTER TO HARIS GHASSANI, KING OF DAMISHQ (DAMASCAS)

In the name of Allah the Compassionate, the Merciful

From Muhammad, Prophet of Allah --

To Haris Bin Abi Shimr

Peace be on him who follows the right path, believes in it and regards it as true.

I invite you to believe in One Allah, who has no associate. Your country would remain with you. [1]

Allah's
Seal: Prophet
Muhammad

Note: Haris, the King of Syria, belonged to Ghassani family

1. *Tabaqat-e-Ibn S'ad, vol. 3, p. 17*

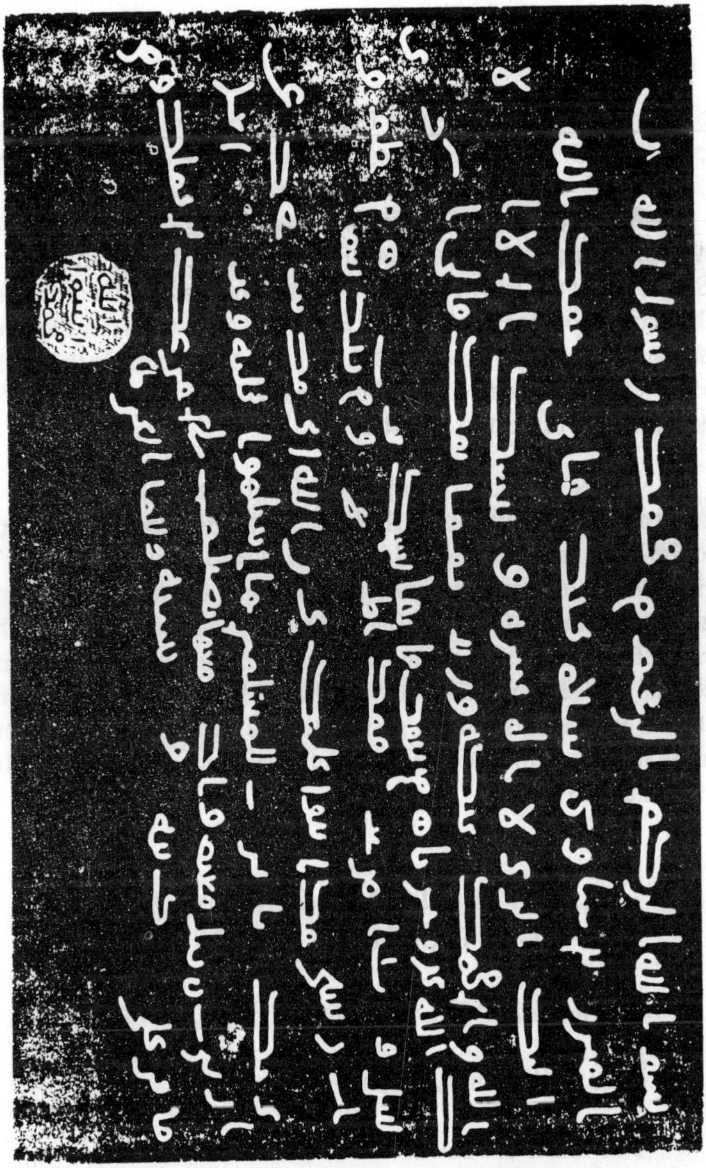

Letter of the Holy Prophet Muhammad (S.A.W.) sent to Munzir bin Sa'wa, Governor of Bahrain

of Arabia, which had settled in Syria towards the end of the 2nd century A.D. and by and by established its rule over the country.

Shuja (R.A.A.) had the honour of taking the letter to Haris, happened to meet Muree, a courtier of the King. Muree enquired of Shuja, about the Holy Prophet (S.A.W.) and was highly moved by the account of the Holy Prophet. He remarked that exactly the same account of the Holy Prophet (S.A.W.) was to be found in the Bible. He, therefore, accepted Islam but warned Shuja, not to mention his acceptance of Islam to any body.

Muree mentioned Shuja to the King, who called Shuja to his court and had the letter read. He was highly infuriated after listening to the letter and said, "who dares even look towards my country"? He ordered his army to make preparations. On his return, Haris gave an account of his meeting to the Holy Prophet (S.A.W.) who said, "In his arrogance of kingship, he has declined to accept Islam, but his rule shall not last". Under the leadership of Caesar, Haris started war against Islam, soon after the victory of Mecca, but ultimately the Ghassani rule was effaced from Syria in the 14th Hijra i.e. 625 A.D.

11. LETTER TO MUNZIR BIN SAWA, GOVERNOR OF BAHRAIN

In the name of Allah, the Compassionate, the Merciful.

From Muhammad, Prophet of Allah —

To Munzir bin Sawa

May peace be on you! I praise Allah, Who is One and there

is none to be worshipped but except Him. I bear evidence to the Oneness of Allah and that I am a servant of Allah and His Prophet.

Thereafter I remind you of Allah. Whoever accepts admonition, does it for his own good.

Whoever followed my messengers and acted in accordance with their guidance; he, in fact, accepted my advice.

My messengers have highly praised your behaviour. You shall continue in your present office. You should remain faithful to Allah and His Prophet.

I accept your recommendation regarding the people of Bahrain. I forgive the offences of the offenders. Therefore, you may also forgive them.

Of the people of Bahrain whoever want to continue in their Jewish or Majusi faith, should be made to pay Jizia.[1]

Allah's
Seal: Prophet
Muhammad

The above letter was written in reply to the following letter of Munzir Bin Sawa:

11.(a) "Allah's Prophet! I received your injunctions. Prior to this, I have also seen the letter, you wrote to the people of Bahrain, extending to them an invitation to Islam. I accept Islam out of my

---

1. *Zadul M'aad, vol. 3, pp. 61—62, Tabaqat Ibn S'ad, vol. 3.*

own will.

Some of the people of Bahrain like Islam and entered the Islamic fold, while others continue in their old faith. In my country, there live Zoroastrians and Jews. You may inform me of the treatment which is to be extended to them".[1]

It may be mentioned here that Bahrain was under the jurisdiction of Iran in the 6th Century A.D. Munzir bin Sawa was the Iranian Governor of Bahrain. The latter received the message of Islam and accepted it.

12. SECOND LETTER TO MUNZIR

In the name of Allah, the Compassionate and the Merciful

Peace be on you. I am sending Abu Huraira and Qudama (R.A.A.) to you. You may hand over to them, whatever amount of Ush'r, Zakat and Jiziya, you have collected in your area.[2]

Allah's
Seal: Prophet
Muhammad

13. LETTER TO JAIFER AND 'ABD, RULERS OF OMAN

In the name of Allah, the Compassionate, the Merciful.

From Muhammad, Prophet of Allah—

To Jaifer and' Abd.

---

1. *Tabaqat Ibn S'ad*, vol. 3, p. 28
2. *Tabqat ibn S"ad*, vol.3. p.19

Peace be on him who adopts the right course. There-after, I invite both of you to Islam. Embrace Islam. Therein lies security! Allah has sent me as a Prophet to his creatures, in order that I may instil fear of Allah in His disobedient creatures and thus there may be left no excuse for those who deny Allah.

My prophethood is about to reach your country. If you two accept Islam, your country will, as usual, remain with you. But if you refuse or object, it is a perishable thing.[1]

Allah's
Seal: Prophet
Muhammad

Note: Jaifer and 'Abd accepted Islam after a slight hesitation and said that the Prophet (S.A.W.), himself acted before ordering others to act and before prohibiting others from a thing, himself abstained from it. They further observed that if he attained victory, he was not proud; and overpowered, he did not deflect from his objective. They further said that the Prophet always fulfilled promises. They testified that he was the Prophet of Allah.[2]

14. LETTER TO THE SUCCESSOR OF AS'HAMA THE NEGUS

In the name of Allah, the Compassionate, the Merciful.

From Muhammad, Prophet of Allah —

To Negus, King of Ethiopia.

---

1. Mawahibe-ludun-niya, vol. 1,p.294, quoted by Al-Wasaiq-us-Siyasa, p. 62.
2. Balagh-e-Mubeen, p. 184

His Prophet (S.A.W.).

I bear witness that there is none to be worshipped except Allah. No one is His associate or partner. He does not stand in need of a wife or children. And I affirm that I am his servant and his Prophet.

I invite you to believe in Allah who is One. If you want security, accept Islam.

O people of the Book! Ignore all matters of difference and dispute, and agree to a thing to which you and we are equally committed, and it is that we should not worship anyone except Allah. And neither should we associate anyone else with Him nor should we regard anyone else as our Sustainer. If they object to it, tell them, "you will bear witness that we believe in Allah."[1]

If you will not accept these, the responsibility of the transgression of your Christian people shall be yours.[2]

Ailah's
Seal: Prophet
Muhammad

The Negus did not accept Islam. He also did not send a reply to the letter.

---

1. In this para, verse 64, from Sura-e-Ale Imran of the Quran has been quoted, which was addressed to the Jews and the Christians.
2. *Risalat-e-Nabaviyya,vp. 291.*

to the letter.

15. LETTER TO THE KINGS OF HIMYAR

In the name of Allah, the Compassionate, the Merciful.

From Muhammad, Prophet of Allah—,

To Haris, etc.

May peace be on you, till you belive in Allah and His Prophet

Undoubtedly Allah is He Who is unique and Who has no associate. he sent Musa (Moses, A.S.) with miracles and created Isa (Jesus, A.S.) by His word. But the Jews say that "Uzair is son of Allah" and the Christians say that Isa (A.S.) is son of Allah and is one out of the three".[1]

Allah's
Seal: Prophet
Muhammad

Note: The Kings of Himyar after listening to the letter, gladly accepted Islam, sent a delegation to the Holy Prophet (S.A.W.) to communicate the news of their acceptance of Islam. The Himyar dynasty ruled over the southern part of Yemen, in the time of the Holy Prophet (S.A.W.). Yemen then comprised the south Western portion of Arabia and its area was over 127 thousand square miles. The two brothers whom the Holy Prophet(S.A.W.)

---

1. *Tabaqat Ibn-e-S'ad, vol. 3, p. 32.*

addressed a letter also ruled over parts of Yemen.

16. SECOND LETTER TO THE KINGS OF THE HIMYAR

The Holy Prophet expressed his deep sense of joy at the acceptance of Islam by the Kings of Himyar and communicated to them injunctions about Zakat and Jizia in the letter that follows:

In the name of Allah, the Compassionate, the Merciful.

From Muhammad, Prophet of Allah,

To Kings of Himyar

May peace be on you. I praise Allah, except Whom there is none to be worshipped.

Your messengers reached here at the time of my return from Room (Byzantium). They delivered your message; related details of your war against the infidels and conditions existing there. Allah has honoured you with His guidance. You should make the obedience of Allah and His Prophet obligatory on you.

Keep saying prayers, paying *Zakat* and fifth of the benefits gained in religious wars, for Allah and His Prophet.

Allah has fixed the payment of charity money on landed property and it is Ushr (One tenth of the produce in rainfed; and canal irrigated lands and in the case of well-irrigated lands, it is at the rate of half Ushr(One twentieth). As *Zakat* per 40 camels one she-camel; per 30 camels, one young camel; per 5 camels a goat and per 10 camels two goats, be given.

A young goat per 40 sheep, and goats. This is the rate of *Zakat* on cattle.

This rate of *Zakat* has been made obligatory on the Muslims. Whoever gives more than this, it is a source of more *Sawab* (Recompense) for him.

But whoever pays the fixed amount; and proclaims his (acceptance of) Islam and helps the Muslims against infidels, is a Muslim. Similarly all the duties and responsibilities of the Muslims shall be applicable to him.

For the fulfillment of this promise, I give the guarantee of Allah and His Prophet.

If a Jew or a Christian embraces Islam, he shall be treated in the same manner. Whoever wishes to continue in Jewish or Christian religion, shall not be forced to change his religion, but he shall have to pay Jiziya, the rate of which for each adult is one dinar,[1] or its equivalent in value, cloth of the same value. Whoever shall pay this amount to the Prophet of Allah (S.A.W.), the responsibility for his protection shall be that of Allah and His Prophet. Whoever refuses Jiziya, shall be regarded as an enemy of Allah and His Prophet.[2]

Allah's
Seal: Prophet
Muhammad

---

1. Dinar was a gold coin and in the present money is equal to a pound sterling.
2. *Tabari's History*, vol. 3, p. 153.

Allah's
Seal: Prophet
Muhammad

17. LETTER TO FARWAH, GOVERNOR OF M'AAN

In the name of Allah, the Compassionate, the Merciful.

From Muhammad, Prophet of Allah—

To Farwah bin 'Amar

Your messenger came to me and delivered the presents you sent me, gave me an account of yourself and conveyed to me the good news of your acceptance of Islam.

Allah has honoured you with His guidance. If you continue to remain obedient to Allah and His Prophet and remain faithful to them, keep saying prayers and paying *Zakat*, it is the greatest blessing of Allah; and take it that Allah has blessed you with His guidance.[1]

Allah's
Seal: Prophet
Muhammad

Note: Farwah had been appointed as Governor of M'aan by the Byzantine government. M'aan which now froms part of Jordan, is situated towards the northwest of Arabia. When Caesar came to know of the acceptance of Islam by Farwah, he reprimanded him and ordered him to give up his new faith, otherwise he threatened to remove him from his office. But Farwah boldly refused. Thereon Caesar imprisoned him, but seeing that even the hardships of the prison could not deflect him from resolution, he ordered that

1. *Tabaqat Ibn S'ad*, vol. 3, p. 31.

Farwah should be put to death. His last words were "Convey the message to the Holy Prophet(peace be on him), that even my bones remained subservient to Allah"

18. LETTER TO 'AMR BIN HAZM ANSARI GOVERNOR OF YEMEN

In the name of Allah, the Compassionate, the Merciful

This writing from the side of Allah the Great and His Prophet, is given to 'Amr bin Hazm Ansari and has been written at the time of his deputation to Yemen.

"Allah, the Sublime has said,
'O faithful ones! Fulfil your promise'

I impress on him that in every matter, he should fear Allah, for "Allah is with those, who fear Him, and take to virtue". I have admonished 'Amr bin Haz'm (R.A.A.) to receive the due to Allah, according to His order. Treat the people with kindness and order them to do good deeds. Teach them the Holy Quran and make them understand the fundamentals of Islam. Only he who is clean, should touch the Quran. The people should be prohibited from evils. They should be made aware of their rights and duties. In ordering them to do good deeds, the people should be treated politely. But there should be no hesitation in taking to task the one who is guilty of oppression and outrage, as Allah, the Sublime does not like cruelty. He has strictly prohibited tyranny. Allah sends curses on tyrants.

People should be informed of the actions and ways which lead to Paradise and warned of the actions which take a person to Hell.

All the people should be treated nicely, in order that they get to understand the elements of the faith adequately.

The tenets of Hajj should also be told in detail in Farz (essentially and obligatory) and *Sunnat* (what is lesser essential, but was done by the Holy Prophet (S.A.W.) should be clearly described. All the commands of Allah in respect of Hajj and Umra should be made known to the people.

People should be prohibited from saying prayers in such clothes, as do not cover the body and during the prayer there is a risk of the private parts being exposed. The instructions in respect of *Wudu* (ablution) should be fully explained. It is ordered that the prayers should be offered at the fixed times and it is directed that the *Ruku* (bowing before Allah during the prayer) should be completely performed. And during the prayers, there should be *Riqqat*(tendency to repent and weep). The *Fajr*(morning) prayers should be said early in the morning (much before sunrise). The *Zuh'r*(early afternoon) prayer should be offered after the sun pasts its zenith and begins to decline. The '*Asr*(late afternoon) prayer offered after the shadow gets oblique. *Maghrib* (evening) prayer should be offered immediately after the sunset, and should not be delayed till the stars appear in the sky. *Isha*(night) prayer should be said in the first part of night.

Regarding Friday prayers, it is ordered that when there is *Azan* (call for prayers), one should immediately leave to say the prayers and before leaving for the Friday prayers, bath taken.

From the goods gained in religious wars, K*hums* (fifth party) be paid, in the way of Allah. From the produce of land of every Muslim, a quantity equal to *Ush'r*(one tenth)should be charged by should be charged half of *Ush'r*(one twentieth).

As for cattle, two goats be taken per 10 camels and four goats per 20 camels. One cow per 40 cows and one calf per 30 cows and one goat per 40 goats.

This rate has been made obligatory on the Muslims, as *Zakat,* by Allah. Whoever pays more, shall deserve greater recompense.

People should not call one another for help in war, in the name of their tribe and family. A person should be helped only for the sake of Allah the One. And whoever invites people to war in the name of tribe or family only instead of Allah, such a rioter should be put to an end.

Invitation to war is only for Allah who is One. If any Jew or Christian embraces Islam of his own free will and with a sincere heart and accepts the way of Allah, he is a Muslim. His rights and duties shall be the same as those of other Muslims.

And whoever continues to adhere to his Jewish or Christian religion, should never be compelled to change his religion. But for each adult of them, a dinar should be levied, which shall be received annually in cash or kind. Cloth of this value can also be accepted.

Whoever refuses to pay this amount, should be regarded as an enemy of Allah, His Prophet and all the Muslims.[1]

Allah's
Seal: Prophet
Muhammad

1. *Tabaris' History,* vol. 3, pp. 156—157

Note: 'Amr (R.A.A.) not only preserved this document, but also collected the other letters of the Holy Prophet (S.A.W.) sent to the different clans, particularly of Jews, Christians and had them bound into a volume. This subsequently served as an authentic source of information, particularly reg. Zakat, Charities, rights of the Muslims and nonMuslims, their duties, etc.

19. LETTER TO UKAIDIR, RULER OF DUMAT-UL-JANDAL

In the name of Allah, the Compassionate, the Merciful.
From Muhammad, Prophet of Allah —

To Ukaidir and people of Duma.

Now that they have embraced Islam and given up idol worship.

The lands of the ponds of Duma, non-agricultural lands, unowned and *nazool* (state property) lands, armours and parts, shall be for us.

All rivers, springs, cultivated lands, trees, grass, etc., shall be the property of the people of Duma.

Zakat shall not be levied on cattle, except those which graze in meadows. Unaccounted for cattle, shall not be included in *Zakat.*

Prayers shall be offered on time, and *Zakat* paid honestly.

faithfulness is assured from our side to which Allah and all the Muslims present, bear witness.[1]

Allah's
Seal: Prophet
Muhammad

Note: Dumatul Jandal, at present known as Jauf, a big caravan centre, is situated half way between Syria and Madina. Kanana, a clan of Arabia lived there. Although the clan was Arab, it had accepted Christianity under the influence of the Roman Empire.Caesar had appointed Ukaidir as the ruler of Duma, on his behalf. Ukaidir embraced Islam gladly and voluntarily.

1. *Tabaqat Ibn S'ad,* vol. 3, p. 36.

PART III

LETTERS AND INJUNCTIONS SENT TO THE CHIEFTAINS, LEADERS AND HEADS OF VARIOUS TRIBES AND INDIVIDUALS

1. LETTERS TO THE POPE OF ROME

In the name of Allah, the Compassionate, the Merciful.

Peace be on him, who believes in Allah. I am of the faith that Isa (Jesus A.S.) son of Mariam (Mary) was the spirit of Allah and His word! Allah infused him in the pious Mariam.

I believe in Allah, all His Books and His Commands which he sent to Me and which He sent to Ibrahim, Ismail, Ishaq and Yaqub (A.S.) and their descendants. I also believe in what was given to Musa and Isa (A.S.) and other prophets by Allah! In faith and belief, we do not differentiate in accepting any of the prophets. We are Muslims (meaning obedient to Allah) Peace be on him who follows the guidance.[1]

Allah's
Seal: Prophet
Muhammad

Note: Alongwith the letter to Caesar, the Holy Prophet

---

1. *Tabari's History,* vol. 3, p. 88.

(S.A.W.) had also sent a letter to the Pope. The latter testified to his Prophethood and observed, "No doubt, he is a true Prophet". Thereafter he addressed a congregation in the cathedral and informed the people that he had received a letter from the Arabian Prophet Ahmad (S.A.W.) who had invited them to accept the true faith of Allah, the One. He then testified that there is no god save Allah and that Ahmad (S.A.W.) was the servant and prophet of Allah. The people were highly infuriated to hear this truthful declaration and they beat him so much that he died.[1]

2. LETTER TO THE JEWS OF KHYBER

In the name of Allah, the Compassionate, the Merciful

From Muhammad, the Prophet of Allah who is like Moosa (Moses A.S.) a prophet and messenger and he testifies to what Moosa (A.S.) had brought.

O people of Torah, has Allah not stated in the Torah that "Muhammad (S.A.W.) is a Prophet of Allah. The people who will be with him, shall be harsh towards the enemies of Allah. And amongst themselves, they shall be kind and loving. They shall bow and prostrate before Allah. And they shall seek His bounty and goodwill".

I ask you to swear by Allah, who sent Torah for you and who made your forefathers eat *'mann,* and '*Salva*' and dried sea for them and rid them of the tyranny of pharaoh. It is not written in Torah that you should believe in me?

---

1. Tabari's Ibn-e-S'ad, vol. 3, p. 28.

After the explanation about me in the Torah, do guidance and transgression become apparent?

Therefore I invite you towards Allah and His Prophet.[1]

Allah's
Seal: Prophet
Muhammad

Note: The Jews and Christians knew well that a prophet would come and they were awaiting his appearance. The Holy Prophet (S.A.W.) was absolutely certain of the prophesy about him in the Torah.

3. LETTER TO BUDAIL BIN WARAQA

In the name of Allah, the Compassionate, the Merciful.

From Muhammad, Prophet of Allah—

To Budail bin Waraqa, etc.

I praise Allah except whom there is no god.

Thereafter, you should know that the people of Tihama are the dearest to me and in relationship are the nearest to me. Whatever I like myself, I like for the one who migrates from amongst you, although he may migrate to a place in his own region.

---

1. *Kanz-ul-Ummal*, vol. 5, p. 285.

shall deserve the same treatment, as the people of Tihama.

I value the people of Tihama and nothing would be done from my side, as is not in accordance with their dignity.

At the time of my treaty with the tribes of Arabia, your people should feel secure.

Alqama son of Ulasa and Houza's two sons have already embraced Islam and both of them have migrated, and have taken *bai' at*(vow) on the same terms as the people of Ikrama have done. We are all equal as regards *Halal*(permissible) and *haram* (forbidden) By Allah, I do not say anything incorrect to you. Allah shall certainly love you.[1]

Allah's
Seal: Prophet
Muhammad

Note: Abdul Muttalib, the grandfather of the Holy Prophet (S.A.W.) had entered into a treaty with the Khuza'a tribe to help each other and descendants of each other. The tribe, therefore, always helped the Holy Prophet (S.A.W.) The tribe informed the Holy Prophet (S.A.W.) of the invasion by the Quraish and the Jews, on Madina.

The tribe lived in the Tihama Valley lying towards the South of Mecca, along the Red Sea and the Serat Mountain. Aslam was a branch of this tribe. Its people presented themselves to the Holy Prophet (S.A.W.) and accepted Islam. The Prophet wrote the following to the tribe.

---

1. Tabaqat Ibn S'ad, vol. 3, p. 25.

4. LETTER TO THE PEOPLE OF ASLAM TRIBE.

In the name of Allah, the Compassionate, the Merciful.

1. Whoever from the Aslam tribe believes in Allah, says prayers, pays *Zakat* and is sincere to the *deen* of Allah, shall be helped, if somebody attacks them.

2. When the Prophet (S.A.W.) needs their help, it shall be obligatory on them to help him.

3. Their villagers shall have the same rights, as those of their citizens.

4. These people can migrate wherever they like.[1]

Allah's
Seal: Prophet
Muhammad

5. LETTER TO THE PEOPLE OF TIHAMA RANGE

In the name of Allah, the Compassionate, the Merciful.

From Muhammad, Prophet of Allah

To the free people of Allah

All those who believe in Allah, offer prayers, and pay Zakat are free from bondage. Muhammad (S.A.W.) is their ruler. They

1. *Tabarqat Ibn S'ad*, vol. 3, p. 24.

shall not be sent back, except to their own tribes and they shall not be answerable for their past crimes. The people from whom their debt is due, shall be made to pay it.

These people shall not be subjected to any oppression or outrage. Whoever embraces Islam, shall be the responsibility of Allah and Prophet Muhammad (S.A.W.) in all the matters mentioned above.

May peace be on you.[1]

Allah's
Seal: Prophet
Muhammad

Note: As mentioned earlier, Tihama is a long valley lying between the Red Sea and Serat Hill. In the mountain range of Tiham lived people belonging to a number of Arabian tribes. They had no regular occupation or calling, but resorted to looting and waylaying. They sent a delegation to the Holy Prophet (S.A.W.) who assured them that their past crimes would be condoned and their slaves would be free.

6. LETTER TO KHALID BIN ZIMAD-UL-AZDI

In the name of Allah, the Compassionate, the Merciful.

The cultivated lands in the possession of Khalid bin Zimad-ul-Azdi at the time of embracing Islam, shall remain his property, provided he believes in Allah, Who does not have an associate, testifies that Muhammad is His servant and Prophet; says prayers, pays *Zakat*, keep fasts of the month of Ramazan and performs Hajj

---

1. *Ibid,* p. 29.

introduces new things in religion, nor doubts the righteousness of Islam; shall remain faithful to Allah and His Prophet; befriend friends of Allah and is hostile to His enemies.

It is obligatory on Prophet Muhammad (S.A.W.) to guard them just as he guards his life and property and that of his kith and kin.

Allah and His Prophet are responsible for Khalid-ul-Azdi, provided there is no disloyalty on his part.[1]

Allah's
Seal: Prophet
Muhammad

Note: Prior to the advent of Islam, Khalid's father Zimad-ul-Azdi, who belonged to Yemen, practised medicine and surgery. During the course of the Prophethood of the Holy Prophet (S.A.W.) he happened to visit Mecca and saw a crowd of street urchins following the Holy Prophet (S.A.W.) and calling him Majnoon(mad). Zimad, thereafter, went to the Holy Prophet (S.A.W.) and informed him that he could cure madness. The Holy Prophet (S.A.W.) spoke a few impressive sentences in praise of Allah, which impressed Zimad to such a degree that he embraced Islam immediately. The Holy Prophet (S.A.W.) wrote the above letter to Khalid.

7. LETTER TO HILAL BIN UMAYYA, CHIEF OF BAHRAIN

In the name of Allah, the Compassionate, the Merciful.

---

1. *Tabaqat Ibn S'ad,* vol. 2, p. 21.

In the name of Allah, the Compassionate, the Merciful.

May peace be on you. I praise Allah who is one and there is no associate of His.

I invite you to believe in Allah, the One. Obey Allah, and enter the fold of Islam. This is the best way for you, and security is for him who follows the straight course.[1]

Allah's
Seal: Prophet
Muhammad

8. LETTER TO USAIBUKHT BIN ABDULLAH, CHIEF OF HAJAR

In the name of Allah, the Compassionate, the Merciful.

From Muhammad, Prophet of Allah

To Usaibukht Bin Abdullah, Chief of Hajar.

Aq'r'a brought your letter and made a recommendation on behalf of your tribe. I have accepted his recommendation. I convey to you the good news that I agree to what you have asked for and what you have demanded, in accordance with your wishes. but to me, it seems reasonable that you explain your demands.

If you come here, you will be honoured. Even if you are unable to come, there is respect for you in my heart.

Although I do not seek any present, but if you want to send

1. *Tabaqat Ibn S'ad,* vol. 3, p. 27.

me a present, I shall gladly accept it.

My workers have spoken of high and esteemed level of your rank. I exhort you to give full regard to prayers, *Zakat* and relationship with the Muslims.

I have proposed the name of Banu Abdullah for your community. You should order your people to say prayers and do good deeds and obtain for yourself the happy news.

May peace be on you and your community of believers.[1]

Allah's
Seal: Prophet
Muhammad

Note: Usaibukht also called Sehbukht, was the Chieftain of Hajar which was, at one time, a big city and is a part of the Arabian province of Al-Hisa and is situated on the Persian Gulf. Usaibukht gladly embraced Islam. The Holy Prophet (S.A.W.) also addressed the following letter to Banu Abdullah.

9. LETTER TO BANU ABDULLAH

In the name of Allah, the Compassionate, the Merciful.

I admonish your people to remain devoted to Allah and not to got astray after receiving guidance and not to lean towards deviation after accepting the right course.

Your delegation has come to me. I have treated it in the manner which pleased it.

---

1. Tabaqat Ibn S'ad, vol. 3, p. 27.

I did not consider it proper to oust you from Hajar. I have accepted the request of your delegation. You should remember the munificence with which Allah has blessed you. I have come to know whatever you people have done. Whoever, from amongst you, will remain faithful, shall not be implicated in the crimes of rioting of others.

When my messengers reach you, do help them in the work of Allah. Whoever from amongst you will perform a virtuous act, his good action will not be overlooked either by Allah, or by me.

Security is for him who follows the right path.[1]

Seal: Allah's Prophet Muhammad

After the conquest of Mecca, the Holy Prophet (S.A.W.) addressed letters which follow, to a number of tribes, many of whom had already accepted Islam.

10. LETTER TO NAHSHALL BIN MAALIK, CHIEF OF BANI VA'IL

In the name of Allah, the Compassionate, the Merciful

From Muhammad, Prophet of Allah

To Nahshall bin Maalik and the people of Bani Va'il, who have already accepted Islam.

All the people should keep on saying prayers; paying Zakat; obeying Allah and His Prophet and paying one fifth out of the

1. *Tabaqat Ibn S'ad*, vol. 3, p. 27.

benefits of holy wars for Allah and His Prophet. Keep on proclaiming acceptance of Islam; and staying away from the infidels. All such people are in the protection and trust of Allah, and Muhammad (S.A.W.) who are responsible for saving them from every kind of oppression and excesses.

Neither shall these people be exiled, nor Ush'r (One tenth) charged from their produce. Their ruler shall be from amongst them.[1]

Allah's
Seal: Prophet
Muhammad

11. LETTER TO RIFA'A BIN ZAID JUZAMI

In the name of Allah, the Compassionate, the Merciful.

From Muhammad, Prophet of Allah

To Rifa'a Bin Zaid.

I am sending Rifa'a to his community. He will extend the invitation of Allah and His Prophet to his community.

Whoever will accept his invitation, shall be taken as belonging to the organization of Allah and His Prophet and whoever will refuse to do so, shall be secure for two months.[2]

---

1. *Tabaqat Ibn S'ad*, vol. 3, pp.33 and 49
2. *Risalate Nabaviyya*, PP. 150-151.

Note: Rifa'a had accepted Islam earlier. The Holy Prophet (S.A.W.) gave him a letter and sent him as a preacher to his tribe.

12. LETTER TO BANU ASAD

In the name of Allah the compassionate, the Merciful

From Prophet Muhammad

To Banu Asad.

Peace be on you. I praise Allah, except Whom there is no god to be worshipped.

Thereafter, you have no right to take over the ownership of the wells and lands of Tai tribe. The use of their wells is not permissible (Halal) for you. Also none shall enter their lands, without their permission.

Whoever will not obey me, shall not be my responsibility.

Qaza'i bin Umar who is their administrator should manage this.[1]

Seal: Allah's Prophet Muhammad

---

1. *Tabaqat Ibn S'ad*, vol. 3, p. 2

13.LETTER TO THE CHIEFS OF AQABA

In the name of Allah the compassionate, the Merciful

From Muhammad, Prophet of Allah

To the People of Aqaba

May peace be on you. I praise Allah who is one and except whom there is nobody else to be worshipped.

I do not intend to wage war against you till you receive my written reason for it. It is better for you, either to accept Islam or agree to pay Jiziya and consent to remain obedient to Allah, His Prophet and his messengers. My messengers deserve honour. Treat them with respect. Whatever pleases my messengers, will also please me.

These people have been informed of the orders about Jiziya. If you desire that there should be peace and security in the world, obey Allah and His Prophet. Thereafter none in Arabia and Ajam (Iran) shall dare cast an evil eye on you. But the rights of Allah and His Prophet can at no time be waived.

If you do not accept these terms and set them aside, I do not need your presents and gifts. In that case, I shall have to wage war (to establish peace and security). Its result would be that the big ones shall be killed in war and the commoners shall be taken prisoners.

I assure you that I am a true Prophet of Allah. I believe in Allah, and His Books, and His Prophets and am of the faith that

Maseeh (Messiah) son of Mariam (Mary), is a Prophet of Allah and His word.

Hurmala (R.A.A.) who brought to me 3 wasaq (about 6 quintals) of barley, recommended your case. Had it not been in compliance of the command of Allah and the good opinion of Hurmala for you, it would not have been necessary for me to correspond with you and instead of it, there would have been a war. If you will obey my messengers, you shall immediately have my support and the help and support of everyone who is attached to me.

My messengers are Shuraih-beel, Obaiy, Hurmala and Hurais (R.A.A.) and whatever decision they take in respect of you, shall be acceptable to me.

Your people are under the protection and responsibility of Allah and His Prophet.

Supply provisions to the Jews of Maqna, for their journey to their country.

If you accept obedience, may peace be on you.[1]

Allah's
Seal: Prophet
Muhammad

Note: As in the present day, Aqaba was an important port of the Red Sea. In ancient times also, due to its being an international trade centre, trade caravans to Palestine and African went through Aqaba and trade goods to the Coastal towns of the Red Sea also came from it. under the influence of the Romans, the local Arab

1. *Tabaqat Ibn S'ad,* vol. 3, pp. 29, 37.

tribes who ruled here, got converted to Christianity, but due to the oppressive behaviour of the Romans, the Arab tribes, living by the side of the Roman frontiers, got hostile to the Romans and wanted to be free.

During the time of the Holy Prophet (S.A.W.), Yuhanna, a bishop, was the ruler of Aqaba. In the beginning he was not prepared to befriend the Muslims. But seeing that Caesar avoided facing the Muslims he came to the side of Islam. Subsequently in the 9th Hijri 630 A.D. the Caesar wanted to invade Madina with a large army. The Holy Prophet (S.A.W.) however, made up his mind to stem the tide of invasion in the country of the enemies. He, therefore, moved his valiant companions to Tabuk, where he waited for the Roman army for about 12 days. The Roman army was highly frustrated by the courage of Muslims and quietly dispersed without fighting. Yuhanna and other heads of the different tribal states sent delegations and assurances of their obedience to the Holy Prophet, who addressed the letter, given above. Yuhanna himself went to the Holy Prophet (S.A.W.) and entered the sanctuary of Islam.

14. LETTER TO THE PEOPLE OF MAQNA

In the name of Allah, the Compassionate, the Merciful.

From Muhammad, Prophet of Allah —

To Bani Janba and People of Maqna

Peace be on you. I have come to know that you are going to your villages. You will be in the security, when this writing reaches you. I have forgiven all your crimes. None shall be allowed to oppress you. For you is the guarantee of Allah and His Prophet. You shall be protected, just as we protect ourselves.

One fourth of the produce of dateplam gardens, Sea-Catch and the Yarn Spun, is due from you. After its payment, you shall be exempt from Jizya and all kinds of free labour. If you will remain loyal, it shall be obligatory on us to honour your respectable people and to forgive all your past offences!

Towards the end of the holy letter, the following direction for the Muslims was written:

Whoever will treat the people of Maqna nicely, it shall be better for him and who ever will maltreat them, it shall be harmful for him.

A ruler for you, shall either be appointed from amongst you or from those connected with me.[1]

Allah's
Seal: Prophet
Muhammad

Note: The people of Maqna which is situated on the Gulf Aqaba, were Jews. They sent a messenger to the Prophet (S.A.W.) assuring him of their loyalty and requested for an injunction.

---

1. *Tabaqat Ibn S'ad,* vol. 3, p. 28.

15. LETTER TO THE PEOPLE OF AZRUH

In the name of Allah, the Compassionate, the Merciful.

From Muhammad, Prophet of Allah

To the people of Azruh

These people are under the refuge and protection of Allah and his Prophet (S.A.W.) In every Rajab (7th month of the Islamic Calendar) one hundred dinars shall be payable by them. Allah shall be their custodian, in return for their goodwill and good turn to the faithful.

These people shall be in every sort of security unless informed otherwise by Muhammad (S.A.W.)[1]

Seal: Allah's
Prophet
Muhammad

16. LETTER TO THE CHIEF OF HAMDAN

In the name of Allah, the Compassionate, the Merciful.

From Muhammad, Prophet of Allah —

To Umair Zimaran

May peace be on you. I praise Allah, except whom there is none to be worshipped.

1. *Maqdisi*, p. 178

Thereafter; On return from Rome, I received the news about the acceptance of Islam by your tribe. Congratulations to the people of the Hamdan that Allah has honoured them with His guidance. Your people should make a declaration of Islam and that there is none to be worshipped except Allah and that Muhammad (S.A.W.) is His Prophet! Those who say their prayers and pay Zakat, shall be the responsibility of Allah and His Prophet. None shall be oppressed, or outraged. And whoever owns something, shall remain owner thereof.

It is not permissible for the Ahle bait (Kins) of the Prophet (S.A.W.) to accept any Charity. Malik bin Musara Ruhawi (R.A.) has delivered your message. I emphasise on you to treat him nicely. He is amongst the best people of his group.[1]

Allah's
Seal: Prophet
Muhammad

Note: The above letter was sent on the occasion of the receipt of the good news that as a result of the preaching of Qais bin Malik who belonged to the Hamdan Tribe, the entire tribe embraced Islam. Earlier Qais had presented himself to the Holy Prophet (S.A.W.) and accepted Islam. He was deputed to preach Islam to his tribe.

17. LETTER TO KHALID BIN WALEED (R.A.A.)

In the name of Allah, the Compassionate, the Merciful.

From Muhammad, Prophet of Allah —

---

1. *Tabaqat Ibne S'ad* vol. 2, pages 73 and 74.

To Khalid bin Waleed.

Peace be on you! I praise Allah except whom there is none to be worshipped.

Thereafter, received your letter, through your messenger, in which you have informed about the acceptance of Islam by Bani Al-Haris. I came to know that they have accepted the invitation which you took to them and that they testify that there is none to be worshipped except Allah, the One, who is without an associate and that Muhammad (S.A.W.) is His servant and Prophet.

Allah has honoured them with His guidance. Give them the good news about Paradise and frighten them from Hell.

After performing this work, come here and tell the people to send a deputation to me.[1]

Peace be on you and
Kindness of Allah and
His blessings

Note: The Holy Prophet (S.A.W.) had sent Khalid bin Waleed (R.A.) to the Bani Haris tribe who lived in Yemen with an invitation to embrace Islam. The entire tribe accepted Islam. When Waleed conveyed the good news the Holy prophet (S.A.W.) wrote to him the above letter.

---

1. *Tabari*, vol. 3, p. 156.

18. LETTER TO MUSAILMA KAZZAB (THE LIAR)

In the name of Allah, the Compassionate, the Merciful.

From Muhammad, Prophet of Allah --

To Musailma Kazzab

Peace be on him, who follows guidance.

Land is that of Allah, Who makes, anyone of his men, whom He desires, its inheritor.

And good ending is for those who fear Allah[1]

Seal: Allah's Prophet Muhammad

Note: It has previously been mentioned that Hauza, the Governor of Yamama had written to the Holy Prophet (S.A.W.) that in case the Prophet was agreeable to include him in his government, he was ready to accept Islam. This demand was rejected by the Holy Prophet (S.A.W.). After the death of Hauza, Musailma succeeded him. Immediately thereafter he falsely declared himself a prophet and wrote to the Holy Prophet (S.A.W.) that he had been associated in the prophethood and therefore, half the country should be given to him. In reply the Holy Prophet (S.A.W.) had a verse of the Holy Quran from Surah A'raf written, translation of which appears above and had it sent to Musailma. Such a brief and yet so eloquent a reply, has no parallel.

1. *Ibid.*, vol. 3, p.167.

Musailma was killed in a battle with Khalid bin Waleed (R.A.A.), after the passing away of the Holy Prophet (S.A.W.).

19. LETTER TO M'UAZ BIN JABAL (R.A.A.)

In the name of Allah, the Compassionate, the Merciful.

From Muhammad, Prophet of Allah —

To M'uaz bin Jabal (R.A.)

May peace be on you! I praise Allah the one. May Allah add to your recompense and calm your sad heart and give you endurance to thank Him.

As a matter of fact, our lives, our kith and kin and our property are merely a trust temporarily reposed in us from amongst the gifts of Allah. He benefits his servant by it, till he likes and when the fixed time comes, He takes it back.

The duty of a man is to thank Allah, when He bestows on him a munificence and when it is taken back, he should endure it with patience.

Your son was a good trust of Allah. He kept you blessed with him, till He liked. And when He desired He took him away from you, in return for a great recompense, provided you keep yourself contented with the will of Allah.

Oh M'uaz (R.A.A.), if you show impatience you will lose your recompense or reward with Allah. If you get to know, how much return and recompense has been granted to you for it, then this loss would appear very meagre in your eye.

The promise which Allah has made with the people who endure misfortune and pain with patience, shall be fully fulfilled in the life to come. The promise of Allah should reduce your grief. Whatever is destined to take place, must occur.

Peace be there![1]

Allah's
Seal: Prophet
Muhammad

Note: M'uaz was an esteemed Companion of the Holy Prophet (S.A.W.) who embraced Islam at the young age of 18. He belonged to the Ansars. The Holy Prophet (S.A.W.) sent him to educate the Muslims, in Yemen while there, his son died. On that occasion the Holy Prophet (S.A.W.) wrote to him the above letter of condolence, exhorting him to bear the loss patiently.

20. LETTER TO GENIE

In the name of Allah, the Compassionate, the Merciful.

This writing of the Prophet of Allah, the Sustainer of the world is for the person who, due to some reason, enters a house at night or resides in a house and inflict harm. O Rahman! bestow goodness on him!

Thereafter! Between us and you, there is an extensiveness

1. *Risalat-e-Nabaviyya*, p. 270.

and room as regards rights. Therefore if you love someone and have a liking for him and do not distinguish between right and wrong and want to resort to force, and belie what is right, then you should know that the Book of Allah gives the right judgement between us and you. Says Allah the Sublime, "This is My Book, which speaks out what is right, as compared to yourself. We record, whatever you do and Our Angles, too keep it writing.

Therefore, let alone the person who has this writing of mine and flee to the idol-worshippers, or go to a person who associates someone else with the worship of Allah although there is none else worthy of worship except Allah. Everything except Him is perishable. In this world, His is the rule and to Him, all have to return (after death)."

"Thaghlaboon" "Ha Meem" They should not be helped. "Ha Meem 'Aen Seen Qaf". The enemies of Allah get dispersed! The proof has already come from Allah. Nobody except Allah wields power and force! Therefore Allah Who is All-Knowing and All-Hearing, is enough to save you from their mischief! [1]

Allah's
Seal: Prophet
Muhammad

Note: Abu Dujana (R.A.) a brave and fearless warrior and a companion of the Holy Prophet (S.A.W.), came to him and related that one night when he lay down on his bed to sleep, he heard a horrible sound and saw something like lightning; and saw a shadow moving in the courtyard. He further mentioned that as he proceeded towards it, a flame leapt in his direction and he was afraid lest it should burn him. The Holy Prophet (S.A.W.) observed that it might

1. Seoti, *Khasa'is-ul-Kubra*, vol. 2, pp. 98, 99.

have been a genie. He, therefore, had the above letter written, which Abu Dujana kept under his pillow and lay down. He heard somebody saying", Oh Abu Dujana, By Lat and Uzza [1] you have burnt me. If you remove the writing from under your pillow, then by the writer of the letter, I shall never visit your house or your neighbour hood again." Abu Dujana related the incident to the Holy Prophet (S.A.W.) Who said, "Abu Dujana! Remove the writing otherwise, by the One Who has sent me as a Prophet, the community of genie shall remain in agony, till the Day of Judgement."

21. LETTER TO ZUL GHUSSA QAIS

In the name of Allah, the Compassionate, the Merciful.

Bani Al Haris and Bani Nahad are the responsibility of Allah and His Prophet (S.A.W.). Neither shall they be ousted from their habitations nor Ushr taken from them, provided they continue to say their prayers, pay Zakat, live apart from infidels and declare their Islam.

Besides these, the protection of roads shall be included among their duties. [2]

Allah's
Seal: Prophet
Muhammad

Note: Zul Ghussa Qais was a Chief of the Bani Nahad Tribe.

---

1. Lat and Uzza were two big idols of Arabia. Lat was installed in Taif and Uzza in the vicinity of Mecca.

2. *Tabaqate Ibne S'ad,* vol. 3, p. [illegible].

22. LETTER TO 'AMR BIN M'ABAD AL-JUHANI

In the name of Allah, the Compassionate, the Merciful.

Whoever from amongst these people accepts Islam, says prayers, pays *Zakat* remains obedient to Allah and His Prophet (S.A.W.), declares his Islam, keeps away from infidels and keeps paying the share of Allah and His Prophet from the benefits of holy wars, shall be in the protection of Allah and His Prophet (S.A.W.)

Whoever from amongst the Muslims, whom payment of a debt is due from somebody, shall receive the amount of the principal only and interest on the pawned amount shall not be admissible.

Zakat on fruits shall be one tenth of the produce.

Whoever will join these people, will have to abide by these injunctions.[1]

Allah's
Seal: Prophet
Muhammad

1. *Tabaqat Ibne S'ad,* vol. 3, p. 24 and 25.

23. LETTER TO BANI ZUHAIR

In the name of Allah, the Compassionate, the Mercifu

From Muhammad, the Prophet of Allah —

To Bani Zuhair

If the people of Bani Zuhair bin Uqaish (a branch of Ukal Tribe), believe in Allah and His Prophet and have faith in them; say prayers, pay *Zakat*, keep away from infidels and accept the share of Allah and His Prophet in the benefits of holy wars; they shall be secure in the protection of Allah and His Prophet.[1]

Seal: Allah's Prophet Muhammad

Note: The above letter was written on a parchment found with a person named Al Namir bin Taulab, who stated it contained the injunctions issued by the Holy Prophet (S.A.W.) to his tribe.

24. LETTER TO SOHAIL BIN 'AMR

In the name of Allah, the Compassionate, the Merciful.

Immediately on receipt of this letter, send me Zamzam[2] water.[3]

Seal: Allah's Prophet Muhammad

---

1. *Tabaqat Ibne S'ad*, vol. 3, p. 22.
2. The name of the Well in the precinct of Harame K'aba.
3. *Risalat-e-Nabaviyya*, p. 154.

Note: As already mentioned elsewhere in this book, Sohail bin 'Amar was a bitter enemy of Islam and made highly inflammable and virulent speeches against the Holy Prophet (S.A.W.). He was the person who made peace with the Holy Prophet (S.A.W.) on behalf of the Quraish on his own terms, after a considerable argumentation. After the conquest of Mecca, he hid himself in his home and requested his son Abu Jundal (R.A.) to have his life spared. An account of the persecution, of Abu Jundal, who had embraced Islam, by his father Sohail, appears elsewhere in this book. The Holy Prophet (S.A.W.) generously forgave all his past faults. Sohail was so moved by the limitless kindness of the Holy Prophet (S.A.W.), that he sincerely embraced Islam and became one of the greatest devotees of Islam. It is well known that none excelled him in saying more prayers, or keeping more fasts and giving more charity. The excess of prayers and fasts extremely emaciated him. As soon as he received the above letter, he sent two water skins of Zamzam Water to the Holy Prophet (S.A.W.)

25. LETTER TO KHAS'AM TRIBE

In the name of Allah, the Compassionate, the Merciful.

O; the people of Khas'am, who live in jungle or villages and who in their dark days (before embracing Islam) committed murders, are forgiven.

Whoever from these people accepts Islam, will have to pay one twentieth of the produce of the land irrigated by springs and one tenth of the produce of rainfed lands.[1]

one tenth of the produce of rainfed lands.[1]

Allah's
Seal: Prophet
Muhammad

Note: The people of Khas'am tribe were agriculturists. The Holy Prophet(S.A.W.) gave general amnesty to the criminals of the tribe in the above letter.

26. LETTER TO ZAMAL BIN 'AMR-AL-UZRI

In the name of Allah, the Compassionate, the Merciful.

I send Zamal bin 'Amr to his people. Whoever embraces Islam, is included in the group of Allah.

And whoever refuses to accept Islam, there is a guarantee for his security too, for two months.[2]

Allah's
Seal: Prophet
Muhammad

Note: Zamal Bin 'Amr, presented himself to the Holy Prophet (S.A.W.) and embraced Islam. The Holy Prophet (S.A.W.) sent him with the above letter, to his people.

---

1. *Tabaqat Ibn S'ad*, vol. 3, p. 34.
2. *Risalat-e-Nabaviyya,* p. 151 and 152.

THE INJUNCTIONS, ORDERS, INSTRUCTIONS, DEEDS ETC. ISSUED BY THE HOLY PROPHET(S.A.W.) TO DIFFERENT HEADS OF TRIBES AND INDIVIDUALS

1. INJUNCTIONS OF THE HOLY PROPHET(S.A.W.) TO 'AMR BIN MURRA JUHANI

In the name of Allah, the Compassionate, the Merciful.

This writing is from Allah, the Sublime, the Great. He disclosed what is right through His Prophet (S.A.W.) and gave him an eloquent Book. 'Amr Bin Murra shall have complete authority over his land. He may graze his cattle, wherever he likes and may water them, provided he keeps paying the fixed *Zakat* in respect of his cattle. There is no *Zakat* on draught cattle.

Allah and all the Muslims testify this agreement.[1]

Note: Amar Bin Murra belonged to Juhaina tribe and owned some land. He had gone to perform Hajj, when one night he saw in a dream, above Kaba a glare which clearly showed the mountains of Madina and Juhaina. He also heard somebody say "Darkness has gone and light has appeared. The last of the Prophets has come; Islam has appeared. Their idols have been shattered and the period of friendship and love has begun." He woke much perturbed. After

---

1. *Kanz-ul-mumal,* quoted by *Risalat-e-Nabaviyya,* p.225—228.

sometime he came to know of the Holy Prophet (S.A.W.) and went to him. The Holy Prophet (S.A.W.) informed him of his prophethood and told him that Islam prohibited unlawful murder, rioting and idolatry and enjoined on them to keep fasts for a month in a year. He further affirmed that the person who accepted these injunctions, would go to paradise and who refused to do so would go to Hell. 'Amr immediately embraced Islam and asked for permission to go to his tribe and preach Islam to them. The people of his tribe except one, embraced Islam. On his return, the Holy Prophet (S.A.W.) gave the above injunctions for the people of his tribe.

2. INJUNCTIONS TO MUTTARIF BIN KAHIN-UL-BAHILI

In the name of Allah, the Compassionate, the Merciful.

From Muḥammad, the Prophet of Allah —

To Muttarif bin Kahin-ul-Bahili

Whoever from your tribe will render cultivable any waste land, that land shall be his.

Such people shall pwes as of *Zakat* a cow per 30 cows; a year old sheep per 40 sheep and one six year old camel per 50 camels.

The collectors of Zakat shall have no right to compel them to receive Zakat from them at any place, other than their meadows. All the people of the tribe are under the protection of Allah.[1]

---

1. *Tabaqat Ibn S'ad*, vol. 3, p. 43, 49

Allah's
Seal: Prophet
Muhammad

3. INJUNCTIONS TO YUHANNA FOR PEACE

In the name of Allah, the Compassionate, the Merciful.

From Allah and Muhammad Prophet of Allah, this letter of peace is for Yuhanna, people of Ela, their scholars; for the boats and caravans which may be on sea and land. Those of the people of Syria Yemen and Seamen who may be with them are also included in this protection. For all of them is the guarantee of Allah and Muhammad, His Prophet! But whoever will violate this promise, shall not be under their protective responsibility.

The water of the wells, where these people stay, shall not be denied to anybody and they will not have a right to block any land or sea routes.[1]

Allah's
Seal: Prophet
Muhammad

Note: The above injunctions were given by the Holy Prophet (S.A.W.) to Yuhanna.

---

1. *Ibid.*, p. 37.

4. DEED GRANTED TO TAMIM-UD-DARI(R.A.A)

In the name of Allah, the Compassionate, the Merciful.

Muhammad, the Prophet of Allah, has conferred the ownership of Baite Habroon, Baite Aenoon, Al Martoom and Baite Ibraheem to Tamim-ud-Dari and his companions. Whatever be therein, shall be theirs.

After them, their descendants shall be their owners.

Whoever will try to deprive them of this ownership, curse of Allah and His angels be on him.[1]

Allah's
Seal: Prophet
Muhammad

Note: Tamimud-Dari, a Christian hermit of Palestine, presented himself, alongwith a man of his tribe, to the Holy Prophet (S.A.W.) and embraced Islam. He was so sure of the righteneous of Islam and its rapid spread, that he requested the Holy Prophet (S.A.W.) to give the ownership deed, in respect of Baite Habroon, etc., although at the time the Quraish had made life for the Holy Prophet (S.A.W.) and his companion miserable and extremely difficult. The Holy Prophet (S.A.W.) was gracious enough to comply with his request. When the latter returned after the battle of Tabuk, Tamim-ud-Dari again presented himself to the Prophet (S.A.W.) and requested for the renewal of the deed. The above document was given in compliance with the request.

---

1. *Tabaqat Ibn S'ad*, vol. 3, p. 75.

5. INJUNCTIONS TO THE TRIBE OF LAKHAM

In the name of Allah, the Compassionate, the Merciful.

1. Whoever from the Tribe of Lakham will embrace Islam, say prayers, pay *Zakat*, pay the *Khums* (fifth) to Allah and His Prophet, keep aloof from the infidels, shall be under the protection and responsibility of Allah, and His Prophet.

2. But whoever will turn his back upon Islam, Allah and His Prophet shall not be responsible for him.

3. If any Muslim will bear testimony to a person's being a Muslim, that person shall be under the protection and responsibility of Muhammad, the Prophet (S.A.W.) and he shall be included amongst the Muslims.[1]

Allah's
Seal: Prophet
Muhammad

6. INJUNCTIONS TO BANI-AL-BAKKA

In the name of Allah, the Compassionate, the Merciful.

From Muhammad, the Prophet —

To Bani-al-Bakka

Whoever from you embraces Islam, says prayers, pays Zakat, remains obedient to Allah and His Prophet (S.A.W.) and his

1. *Tabaqat Ibn S'ad*, vol. 3, p. 37.

companions, pro-claims his Islam and severes connection with infidels, is under the security of Allah, the Sublime and Great and His Prophet (S.A.W.)[1]

Allah's
Seal: Prophet
Muhammad

Note: A three-man deputation of Bani-al-Bakka, including M'uavia bin Saur, presented itself to the Holy Prophet (S.A.W.). Ibn Saur requested the Holy Prophet (S.A.W.) to bless his son Bishr. The Prophet (S.A.W.) passed his hand over the face of Bishr and prayed for their prosperity. It is stated that never did the Tribe, which usually faced famines, had famine in their area and were always prosperous, thereafter.

7. TO BANI UQAIL

In the name of Allah, the Compassionate, the Merciful.

This certification of Muhammad, Prophet of Allah is for Rabi, Muttarif and Anas.

These people are given the land of Aqiq Valley. Till they continue to say prayers, pay *Zakat* and remain obedient to Allah and His Prophet (S.A.W.), they shall be entitled to receive benefit from the Aqiq valley.[2]

---

1. *Ibid.*, vol. 3, P. 45.
2. *Tabaqat Ibn S'ad*, vol. 3, p. 45.

Allah's
Seal: Prophet
Muhammad

Note: A deputation of the Uqail Tribe presented itself to the Holy Prophet (S.A.W.) and embraced Islam. The Holy Prophet (S.A.W.) gave them a tract of land in Aqiq Valley. Another delegation of Bani Uqail received a watering place named Nozaim.[1]

Allah's
Seal: Prophet
Muhammad

8. LETTER TO BANI UQAIL

In the name of Allah, the Compassionate, the Merciful.

This certification of Muhammad, Prophet of Allah is for Rabi, Muttarif and Anas.

These people are given the land of Aqiq Valley. Till they continue to say prayers, pay Zakat and remain obedient to Allah and His Prophet (S.A.W.) they shall be entitled to receive benefit from the Aqiq Valley.[2]

Allah's
Seal: Prophet
Muhammad

1. *Tabqat ibn S'ad*, vol. 3, p. 45.
2. *Ibid.*, p. 45.

9. TO BARIQ TRIBE

In the name of Allah, the Compassionate, the Merciful.

From Muhammad, Prophet of Allah (S.A.W.)

To the People of Bariq

None shall pluck the fruits produced by the people of Bariq, except with their permission. It shall not be permissible to graze cattle in their meadows in any season of winter and summer. However, if any Muslim, not having a meadow, passes through their land with cattle for grazing them, it shall be the responsibility of the people of Bariq to entertain him for three days at the maximum. When fruits in their gardens ripen, a traveller shall be entitled to pick and eat as many fallen fruit as can satisfy his hunger, but he shall not be entitled to carry the fruit with him.[1]

Allah's
Seal: Prophet
Muhammad

10. TO ZUR'A ZI YAZAN

In the name of Allah, the Compassionate, the Merciful.

From Muhammad, the Prophet of Allah—

To Zur'a Zi Yazan

---

1. *Tabaqat Ibn S'ad*, vol. 3, p. 81.

I declare that there is none to be worshipped except Allah and I am his servant and Prophet.

When my messengers Ma'az Bin Jabal, Abdullah Bin Zaid, Malik Bin Ibada, Aqaba Bin Nimr, Malik Bin Murara and Theri companions reach there, you should welcome them and hand over to them *zakat* and *Jiziya* after collecting these.

Malik Bin Murara has reported to me that from amongst the Zumair Tribe, you have embraced Islam first of all, and that you have been fighting against the infidels. For this, I give you the good news of blessings and I impress upon you to do good to. your subjects. Neither should they be treated dishonestly, nor their help withdrawn.

The Prophet of Allah must be obeyed by all, rich or poor. It is not permissible for him or any of his kins to accept charity. Zakat which is received, is for the indigent Muslims, and travellers and that its payment is meant to cleanse wealth.

The people whom I have sent to you, are good followers of mine, by virtue of their knowledge and actions. Therefore, they deserve your good treatment.[1]

Peace be on you and kindness of Allah and His blessings.

Allah's
Seal: Prophet
Muhammad

---

1. Tabari's History, vol. 3, p. 153—154.

11. TO THE CHIEFS OF 'ABAHILA, HADAR MAUT

In the name of Allah, the Compassionate, the Merciful.

From Muhammad, Prophet of Allah —

To Chiefs of Abahila

You should keep saying prayers and paying *Zakat*. It is obligatory and necessary for every one from whom *Zakat* is due, to pay *Zakat* on the cattle, which have been grazing in meadows for the major part of a year.

As regards *Zakat*, it is not right to cheat the collector in order to escape *Zakat* or get it reduced.

It is also your responsibility and obligation to help the Islamic army with provisions. And for every group of ten men, to provide a camel-load of grains is essential.

The person who hides his wealth shall be saving his money in this manner, he like a usurer who lives on interest.[1]

Allah's
Seal: Prophet
Muhammad

Note: Due to the intensive efforts of Hazrat Ali, Mu'az Bin Jabal and Abu Musa (R.A.A.) whom the Holy Prophet (S.A.W.)

---

1. *Risalat-e-Nabaviyya,* p. 295, 297.

had sent to Hadar Maut, the entire population of Yemen got converted to Islam. When Wa'il, a chief of Hadar Maut presented himself to the Holy Prophet, he blessed him and gave the above injunction for his people.

In another order the Holy Prophet (S.A.W.) stated the rate of *Zakat* and punishment for lechery. Its text was as follows:

12. *In the name of Allah the Compassionate, the Merciful*

1. An average goat as Zakat per 40 goats is essential.

2. On the material which is obtained from the mines, one fifth should be paid.

3. A person who violates the modesty of a virgin, shall be given 100 lashes and exiled for one year. And the person who is guilty of adultery with a married woman, should be stoned to death.

4. There must not be a shame or indolence (in executing) whatever Allah has made obligatory.

5. Every intoxicant is forbidden.

6. Wa'il Bin Hujar has been appointed as Governor of all the people of Hadar Maut.[1]

Allah's
Seal: Prophet
Muhammad

1. *Risalat-e-Nabaviyya*, p. 295, 297.

13. TO WA'IL BIN HUJAR

In the name of Allah, the Compassionate, the Merciful.

From Muhammad, Prophet of Allah—

To Wa'il Bin Hujar

As you have embraced Islam, I, therefore, let all your property and forts remain in your ownership. You shall, as usual, own them all.

However, you will have to give one tenth of the produce (*'Ushr*). The decision regarding the division shall be jointly made by two judges. Steps will be taken to see that oppression of no sort is committed against you, till the establishment of the rule of the religion.

Allah's Prophet and all the Muslims are your helpers in this matter.[1]

Allah's
Seal: Prophet
Muhammad

Note: Wa'il had complained to the Holy Prophet (S.A.W.) that his relatives had illegally taken possession of much of his landed property. The Holy Prophet (S.A.W.) promised to give him much more than his demand and gave him the above orders. However, Wa'il was soon fed up with the worldly pomp and preferred to the Holy Prophet (S.A.W.) personally and was ultimately a prominent companion of the Holy Prophet (S.A.W.). To

1. *Tabaqat Ibn S'ad*, vol. 3, p. 25, 79.

those who grasp the real meaning of this life, temporal glamour becomes meaningless.

14. TO THE CHIEFS OF YEMEN

In the name of Allah, the Compassionate, the Merciful.

From Muhammad, Prophet of Allah—

To Shuraihbeel and Haris, etc.

Your messenger reached here with *Khums* (one-fifth of the benefit of the Holy wars), sent by you.

Allah has fixed '*Ushr* ' on the produce of rainfed land and fruits of gardens. But '*Ushr* on fields and gardens which are irrigated, is half (20th part or 5%) provided in both the cases, the quantity of the produce comes to five *wasaq* (about two quintals of the present day).

The rate of *Zakat* on camels and goats is:

1. On every five camels upto 24, grazing on meadows, one goat be given.

2. From 25 to 35, one binte *makhaz* (the young one of camel, which has entered the second year of life) be given.

3. From 36 to 45, one *binte laboon* (the young camel which has entered the third year) be given.

4. From 46 to 60, one *hiqqa* (he/she camel which has entered

fourth year) be given

5. From 61 to 90, one *Jiz'a* (one he/she camel which has entered fifth year) be given

6. From 91 to 120, two *hiqqas* be given

7. On more than 120 camels, one *binte laboon* on every 40 additional camels and on every 50 additional camels one *hiqqa* is fixed.

8. On the goats grazing on meadows, *Zakat* from 40 to 120 goats, is one goat.

9. From 121 to 200, two goats.

10. From 201 to 300, three goats be given and likewise on every 100, one goat be added.

11. Useless, deformed and old cattle should not be given in *Zakat*.

12. To avoid *Zakat*, the cattle of two persons should neither be combined nor separated.

13. One every 5 auqias[1] of silver, the obligatory *Zakat* is 5 *dirham* and on less than 5 auqias, there is no Zakat.

14. On more than five *auqias*, *Zakat* is one *dirham* on every 40 *dirhams*.

---

1. *Auqia = 40 dirhams and a dirham* is about 1/10 th of an ounce.

15. On gold, on every 40 *di*nars,[1] one *dinar* is obligatory

16. It is not admissible for Muhammad (S.A.W.) and his kins to accept *Sadaqa* (charity) and *Zakat*. It is for the poor travellers, etc. only.

17. To associate someone with Allah, to kill a sinless Muslim, to avoid *Jihad* (holy war), to disobey parents, to falsely accuse a sinless person, to learn magic, to take interest and to grab the property of an orphan, are the major sins in the eyes of Allah.

18. None should touch the Quran without cleansing himself.

19. The *Umra* of the House of Allah, is a smaller *Hajj*.

20. There can be no divorce before *nikah* (formal marriage). In order to set a slave free it is essential first to purchase to him.

21. Prayers should not be offered in a cloth which cannot cover the entire body. It is not permissible (for a woman) to say prayers, after tying her hair, in the shape of a hump.

22. Whoever will murder a *momin* (true believer) *qisas* (death punishment) shall be imposed on him, but if the heirs of the murdered person agree to accept *diat* (blood money), 100 camels shall be given as compensation for the murder. Compensation for eyes, lips, backs, tongues and private parts, is the same.

---

1. Dinar, a gold coin, is equivalent of the present day pound.

23. Compensation for a foot is 50 camels. The same is the compensation for *mamuma* (the wound of skull which penetrates to the membrane of the brain). Compensation for *jaefa*(wound of belly) is one third. The compensation of the wound, inflicted with a stick is 15 camels and that for the fingers of hand or foot, is 10 camels for each finger. And for each tooth, the compensation is 5 camels. Compensation for *muzeha*(the wound of head, which exposes skull) is also 5 camels.

In the qisas of a woman, the murderer whether man or woman, shall be put to death.

This is the rate of compensation for the common men. A wealthy person will have to pay one thousand dinars, as compensation.[1]

Allah's
Seal: Prophet
Muhammad

Note: It has been mentioned elsewhere that the Holy Prophet (S.A.W.) had sent 'Amar Bin Hazm Ansari as Governor of Yemen. At that time he sent the above injunctions to his administrators Shuraih-beel and Haris.

1. *Risalat-e-Nabaviyya*, p. 155 and 156.

15. INJUNCTIONS TO YAZEED BINAL-MUHAJJAL HARISI

In the name of Allah, the Compassionate, the Merciful.

The place of Nimra and its means of irrigation and Wadi Ar-Rahman in the jungle of Nimra, shall remain in his ownership.

Yazeed and after him, his successors shall be the chiefs of their tribe Bani Malik. Neither shall war be waged against them, nor shall they be ousted from their colonies.

Written by Mugheera Bin Sh'oba.[1]

Allah's
Seal: Prophet
Muhammad

Note: The above injunctions were issued to the delegation of Bani Al-Haris which visited the Holy Prophet (S.A.W.) under the leadership of Yazeed Al-Harisi.

16. TO BANI MUAVIYA BIN JARWAL

In the name of Allah, the Compassionate, the Merciful.

Whoever from these people embraces Islam says prayers, pays Zakat, obeys His Prophet (S.A.W.), pays Khums to Allah and His Prophet (S.A.W.), out of the holy wars benefits and declares his

1. *Tabaqat Ibn S'ad*, vol. 3, p. 22.

Islam, is under the protection of Allah and His Prophet (S.A.W.). Whatever is with them at the time of the acceptance of Islam, shall be theirs. Upto whatever point the sheeps reach while grazing, they shall be regarded as owners of the land upto that point.[1]

Allah's
Seal: Prophet
Muhammad

17. ORDERS TO DHUMAIRA LAISI

In the name of Allah, the Compassionate, the Merciful.

This writing of Muhammad, Prophet of Allah is for Dhumaira Laisi.

The Prophet of Allah (S.A.W.) has set free from slavery, Dhumaira Laisi. Now he is absolutely free. If he desires to stay with the Prophet of Allah (S.A.W.) he can do so. And if wishes to go to his family, he can go there.

No person should interfere with him in any way except in so far as the rights of Allah and rights of men, are concerned. And whichever Muslim meets him, should treat Dhumaira nicely.[2]

Allah's
Seal: Prophet
Muhammad

---

1. *Tabaqat Ibn S'ad*, vol. 3, p. 23
2. *Isti'ab*, vol. 1, p. 229.

Note: Once the Holy Prophet (S.A.W.) found a woman weeping. He stopped and enquired of her the reason of her grief. The woman informed him that her son was made a slave and sold. She further stated that as he was the only support of her life, she was weeping. The Holy Prophet (S.A.W.) was much moved by her story. He immediately sent a person and purchased Dhumaira from his master, set him free and issued the above orders.

18. INJUNCTIONS TO BANI NAHAD

In the name of Allah, the Compassionate, the Merciful.

Peace be on him who believes in Allah and His Prophet

Whichever person says prayers, is a *momin* (faithful) and whoever pays Zakat is a Muslim. And whoever affirms Oneness of Allah and believes in His Prophet, shall not be counted as a delinquent in the eyes of Allah.

You shall have full rights of the use of your meadows and none shall cut down your trees. Leniency shall be shown in the collection of *Zakat* from you, but sick, old cattle should not be given in *Zakat*.

Whoever will adhere to this promise, it shall be obligatory on the Holy Prophet (S.A.W.) to help him. And whoever will violate this promise it would be an excess on his part.[1]

Allah's
Seal: Prophet
Muhammad

---

1. *Risalat-e-Nabaviyya*, p. 105—107

19. ORDER TO 'ABD YAGHOOS AL-HARISI

In the name of Allah, the Compassionate, the Merciful.

While in possession of cultivable lands, Abde Yaghoos Al-Harisi embraced Islam, those lands, all their things and datepalm gardens, etc., shall remain with him and the people of his tribe, who will obey and follow Abde Yaghoos.

Till these people continue to say their prayers, pay *Zakat* and pay *Khums* from the benefits of holy wars, neither *'ushr* on the produce of their lands shall he charged, nor shall they be dispossessed of their lands.[1]

Allah's
Seal: Prophet
Muhammad

20. ORDERS TO RABI'A BIN ZI-MARHAB AL-HADRAMI

In the name of Allah, the Compassionate, the Merciful.

The wealth and goods of these people, their slaves, wells, canals, villages, trees, the grass of jungle, which grows in Hadar Maut, shall be for the family of Zi-Marhab.

The canal with which these people carry out irrigation, and which flows upto Ale Qais, shall be theirs.

The produce of gardens which are pawned with them, shall

---

1. *Tabaqat Ibn S'ad*, vol. 3, p. 221

be the right of the person who pawned them. The pawnee can not draw profit from the pawned thing. Allah and His Prophet (S.A.W.) shall have nothing to do with the one who contravenes this. It shall be obligatory on the Muslims to help the family of Zi-Marhab. It shall be imperative on the Muslims to save them from loss of life and property. Allah and His Prophet (S.A.W.) are their helpers.[1]

Allah's
Seal: Prophet
Muhammad

21. INJUNCTIONS TO THE KALB TRIBE

In the name of Allah, the Compassionate, the Merciful.

From Muhammad, Prophet of Allah —

To Bani *Jinab* of the Kalb Tribe and his helpers.

It is obligatory on those who say their prayers, pay *Zakat*, keep their faith firm and exert themselves in fulfilling their promises, to give by way of *Zakat* one goat on every five goats, which are tended by a goat herd and a faultless she camel on 50 she camels, whose young ones die.

No *Zakat* shall be levied on load bearing animals on the land which is irrigated by canal, and half '*Ushr* on the rainfed land is to be paid.

The cattle which stray into their area, shall be theirs. No more than the fixed amount shall be charged from them.

---

1. *Ibid.*, p. 21.

Allah and His Prophet are responsible for this writing.

Allah's
Seal: Prophet
Muhammad

22. INJUNCTIONS TO MEHRI BIN AL-ABYAD

In the name of Allah, the Compassionate, the Merciful.

1. The colonies of the true Muslims of Mehra Tribe shall not be devastated or ruined. Neither could they be invaded, nor war waged against them.

2. It is incumbent on these people to act according to the commandments of the religion.

3. A lost thing will have to be restored to its owner.

4. The cattle shall not be kept thirsty.

5. Disobedience, impolite talk and bloodshed should be avoided.

6. Any person who will abide by these injunctions, shall be the responsibility of Allah and His Prophet (S.A.W.) and the violator shall be considered, as if waging war against Allah.[1]

Allah's
Seal: Prophet
Muhammad

---

1. *Tabaqat Ibn S'ad*, vol. 3, p. 34.

Note: A delegation of the Mehra Tribe went to the Holy Prophet (S.A.W.) under the leadership of Mehri bin Abyad and embraced Islam. The above injunctions were given to them on that occasion.

23. INJUNCTIONS TO 'AMIR BIN ASWAD TAI

In the name of Allah, the Compassionate, the Merciful.

From Muhammad, Prophet of Allah —

To 'Amir Bin Aswad Tai

The colonies, wells and springs of 'Amir and his tribe Tai, shall remain in their possession, provided they keep saying prayers and paying *Zakat*, and remain aloof from the infidels.

Written by Mugheera.[1]

Allah's
Seal: Prophet
Muhammad

24. INJUNCTIONS TO HABIB BIN 'AAMAR AL-TAI

In the name of Allah, the Compassionate, the Merciful.

The wealth, lands and residential property and wells of any person, who embraces Islam and says prayers, shall remain in his ownership. None of his articles shall be taken possession of Allah

1. *Tabaqat Ibn S'ad*, vol. 3, p. 34.

and His Prophet(S.A.W.) are responsible for this writing.[1]

Allah's
Seal: Prophet
Muhammad

Note: The above two injunctions were issued by the Holy Prophet (S.A.W.) to the two chiefs of the Tai tribes, when they presented themselves to the Holy Prophet (S.A.W.), and requested for the restoration of the rights of their property. The tribe is well known throughout the world on account of Hatim Tai, whose charity was boundless.

25. ORDERS TO BANI JUWAIN

In the name of Allah, the Compassionate, the Merciful.

From Muhammad, Prophet of Allah—

To Bani Juwain

Whoever from Bani Juwain believes in Allah, says prayers, pays Zakat, keeps away from infidels, remains obedient to Allah and His Prophet, continues to pay the share of Allah and His Prophet and adheres firmly to Islam, every such person is the responsibility of Allah and His Prophet (S.A.W.).

The lands, wells and all those things which they possessed and used legally, shall remain in their ownership.[2]

---

1. *Tabaqat Ibn S'ad*, vol. 3, p. 23.
2. *Tabaqat Ibn S'ad*, vol. 3, p. 22.

Allah's
Seal: Prophet
Muhammad

26. DEED GRANTED TO ZUBAIR BIN AWWAM

In the name of Allah, the Compassionate, the Merciful.

From Muhammad, Prophet of Allah

To Zubair Bin Awwam

I have granted the entire land of Shawaq to Zubair. None shall interfere with him.

Written by Ali (R.A.A.)

Allah's
Seal: Prophet
Muhammad

Note: Zubair (R.A.A.) was a cousin (son of his father's sister) of the Holy Prophet (S.A.W.), and embraced Islam at an early age of 16. The Holy Prophet used to say that every prophet had Hawari (apostles) and that Zubair was his apostle. He was the person who participated in all the holy wars. The Holy Prophet (S.A.W.) granted him an estate, as in the above deed.

27. DEED GRANTED TO AUSAJA BIN HURMALA JUHANI

In the name of Allah, the Compassionate, the Merciful.

The Prophet of Allah (S.A.W.) has granted the land of Zil-Marwah to Ausaja Bin Hurmala. This document is for the same. He (S.A.W.) has bestowed on him the entire piece of land from Balkasa to Musn'a and from Jafalat to the boundary of Jabal-e-Qibla. None shall interfere with him in this respect. Whoever disputes with him in the matter, shall not be in the right.[1]

Allah's
Seal: Prophet
Muhammad

28. ORDERS TO BANI JURMUZ

In the name of Allah, the Compassionate, the Merciful.

The people of Bani Jurmuz will have peace and security in their colonies. Whatever wealth and property they had at the time of the acceptance of Islam, shall remain in their ownership.[2]

Written by Mugheera (R.A.A.)

Allah's
Seal: Prophet
Muhammad

---

1. *Tabaqat Ibn S'ad*, vol. 3, p. 26.
2. *Tabaqat Ibn S'ad*, vol. 3, p. 24.

29. DEED GRANTED TO BANI SHAMAKH

In the name of Allah, the Compassionate, the Merciful.

This is the deed, which Prophet Muhammad (S.A.W.) has granted to Bani Shamakh of Juhaina Tribe. I have given to them the land of Sufaina, which they have marked and begun cultivation. None shall interfere with them.[1]

Written by Aqaba(R.A.A.)

Allah's
Seal: Prophet
Muhammad

30. DEED GRANTED TO BANI AL-HARIS

In the name of Allah, the Compassionate. the Merciful.

Saria and its high land have been given to Bani Al-Haris, provided they say prayers, give Zakat keep away from infidels, and remain faithful and obedient to Allah and His Prophet (S.A.W.)[2]

Allah's
Seal: Prophet
Muhammad

---

1. *Tabaqat Ibn S'ad* , vol. 3, p. 24.
2. *Tabaqat Ibn S'ad*, vol, 3, p.22.

31. DEED GRANTED TO BILAL BIN HARIS AL-MUZANI

In the name of Allah, the Compassionate, the Merciful.

Al-Nahal, Juz'a, etc. have been given to Bilal AL-Muzani. In addition, Al-Muzza and Ghaila are granted to them. The high and low lands of all these places shall be theirs. They shall also own the the mines, which are situated in these lands, provided they adhere firmly to Islam.[1]

Seal: Allah's Prophet Muhammad

32. DEED GRANTED TO HIRAM BIN ABD-AS-SULAMI

In the name of Allah, the Compassionate, the Merciful.

Hiram Bin Abd is granted 'Izama and the part of Shawaq which is his, is allowed to remain with him. Neither shall anyone commit an oppression or excess on him in this respect, nor will these people be allowed to outrage or tyrannise others. [2]

Written by Khalid bin Sa'ed.

Seal: Allah's Prophet Muhammad

---

1. *Tabaqat Ibn S'ad*, vol.3,p.25.
2. *Tabaqat Ibn S'ad*, vol.3, P.26.

33. DEED GRANTED TO SA'EED BIN SUFYAN

In the name of Allah, the Compassionate, the Merciful.

This document is an instrument by virtue thereof the Prophet of Allah (S.A.W.) has granted the datepalm garden of As-Swaraqia to Saeed Bin Sufyan As-R'ali. None shall question him in this regard.

Written by Khalid Bin Saed.[1]

Seal: Allah's Prophet Muhammad

34. DEED GRANTED TO 'UTBA BIN FARQAD

In the name of Allah, the Compassionate, the Merciful.

By virtue of this deed, the Prophet (S.A.W.) has granted land near the Mount of Marwa in Mecca for the construction of a house, to Utba Bin Farqad. None shall interfere with him in this respect.[2]

Written by M'uaviya

Seal: Allah's Prophet Muhammad

---

1. *Tabaqat Ibn S'ad*, vol. 3, p. 34.
2. *Tabaqat Ibn S'ad*, vol. 3, p.34.

EPILOGUE

I wish to conclude this compilation with an expression of highest gratitude and thanks to Allah, who enabled me to translate the letters, treaties, pacts, injunctions and orders of the Holy Prophet Muhammad (S.A.W.) for the benefit and guidance of the people who speak or understand English. May Allah in His infinite Mercy and Benevolence, condescend to favour this humble effort, with His kind approval. The aim of the Holy Prophet (S.A.W.) was to convey the message of Allah, to all the people of Arabia and contiguous and far off countries, different emperors, kings, vice-gerents, governors, chieftains, leaders, etc. and to invite them to accept Islam. Similarly the object of this humble compilation is to communicate the guidance of Holy Prophet of Allah (S.A.W.) to as many people as possible and to apprise them to their real duties and responsibilities. Then, on the Day of Judgement, they will not be able to put forward the excuse that nobody informed them of the teachings of Islam, which only point to the correct and true way of life. Thousands and thousands of prophets (A.S.) were sent by Allah, to bring the transgressors back to the straight course.

When due to the instigation of Satan, Adam (A.S.) committed the first sin, against which Allah had forewarned him, he, with his wife, was ordered to go out of Paradise, as a punishment. After being pardoned by Allah, they were sent to earth. Allah, however, told them that whoever would act upon whatever guidance was sent to them by Him, would have neither fear, nor sorrow. [1] This was meant for the descendants of Adam (A.S.). Therefore, whenever mankind went astray, prophets were sent to keep them on to the right track. Neither did any prophet contradict any other prophet,

---

1. *Holy Quran*, 2:38.

who came before him, nor did any Book of Allah go against any other Book of His. None of the prophets introduced any new religion. Accordingly, the Holy Quran clearly states:

> "We sent Torah, in which there was guidance and light. The prophets who were Muslims, decided all the matters of the people, who had turned Jews, in accordance with it (Torah). Similarly did the saintly people and the religious scholars, as they were made responsible to guard the Book of Allah and they were witness to it.."
>
> (5:44)

In verse 46 of the same Surah, it is again stated:

> "And after them, we sent Isa, son of Mariam (A.S.) who testified to the correctness of Torah, the Book which was sent before him. And we gave him Injeel, in which there was guidance and light and which testified to the truth of the Book sent before, namely Torah. And it is altogether a guidance and admonition." (5:46).

The Holy Quran reiterates that of all the prophets whom Allah sent, there was none, who contradicted the teachings of his predecessors or who introduced his own religion. Similarly Allah did not sent any of the Books, which contained anything contrary to the earlier Books. As a matter of fact, each Book of Allah confirmed the previous Books. The author or sender of the Books being One; their aim and object must be one. So should their teachings be.

It was a sense of false pride and importance, which made certain people call themselves Jews, Christians, etc. Allah did not create such distinctions, otherwise He and His Prophets (A.S.) would have given indications thereof. If the origin, progress and vicissitudes of the Jewish and Christian religions and the life and work of Musa and Isaa (A.S.) are minutely and closely studied, it would be found that both the religions did not have the appellations they now have, for a very long period of time, at least not during the life time of the two prophets. This obviously shows that they did not intend to give any other name except Islam to their teachings. Similarly none of the prophets claimed any relationship with Almighty Allah, as He does not stand in need of any relatives and does not require any help or succour from anybody, for any work. He is One and Omnipotent.

Oneness of Allah and His Omnipotence is one of the most important and distinctive features of Islam. All other religions, either associate someone else with Allah or divide Him into many gods, and this is what is the real source of conflict, confusion and trouble. Obviously difference of opinion and confusion is the essential and natural consequence of the division of responsibility, in any sphere of activity. If there is a clash at the very source of power and authority, the entire field of activity falling under the jurisdiction of that authority, is bound to be thrown into chaos and confusion. Islam, therefore, regards Shirk (association of someone else with Allah) as the greatest and most heinous sin. It, most emphatically and vehemently, establishes that "THERE IS NO GOD EXCEPT ALLAH AND MUHAMMAD IS HIS PROPHET." Without a firm belief in this, no one can be a Muslim.

Human vanity, false pride, exaggerated opinion of wisdom and capabilities, wealth and high position have often stood in the way of believing in Allah, His Prophets and His Books. Nimrod regarded himself as a god simply because he could get an innocent man killed and set free a criminal. Most of the prophets were ridiculed by men of rank and position. Their faulty and perverted minds lead them into thinking that the entire world came into being of itself or haphazardly or by chance. It is really unbelievable that a thing which itself came into existence just haphazardly, could possibly develop clockwork accuracy, precision and regularity. The Holy Quran, time and again, refers to the wonders created by Allah, in the shape of th sun, the moon, the stars, hills, seas, rivers, rain, water, fertile lands, fruits, food grains, flowers, vegetables, animals, cattle and countless such objects. Can men with all their combined efforts create even a tiny live object, like a fly or a mosquito. It is, therefore, not reasonable that instead of putting up with a mere conjecture that the world came into existence just by chance or through interaction of some elements; one should believe in Allah, who created all things, with a purpose and not playfully.

Just as some people do not believe in Allah, they doubt the veracity of the Books of Allah. During the early period of the rise of Islam, the Arabs stated that the Holy Prophet (S.A.W.) had himself produced the Quran. Allah, the Sublime Himself refuted this assertion and challenged them produce a small surah like that of the Quran and to summon their helpers to assist them in the task. It may not be out of place to mention in this connection that the Arabs considered themselves highly accomplished and skilled literary and rhetorical poets and writers and regarded others as dumb, but they were unable to pick up the gauntlet. Does it stand to reason that a person who did not absolutely know reading and writing, however, capable or sagacious he might have been, could compile a book like the Holy Quran, which contains guidance and light for the entire mankind, for all times to come; which besides being an exquisite and inimitable piece of highest noblest literature, contains brilliant jewels of counsel and injunction on how to live in this temporal home in a spirit or brotherly love and in blissful peace and tranquility. It also relates in beautiful style, for the benefit of mankind, tales of transgression, callousness, unreasonable hatred and despicable behaviour of the people towards the prophets of their times. As a result of their misdoings the wrath of Allah visited them in the shape of earthquakes, horrible thunderstorms, famines, pestilences and above all the Deluge, which laid waste the earth. Despite the severe punishment of Allah, mankind continued to tread the path of evil and sin and continues to do so.

As in the case of the Holy Scriptures, mankind belied the Prophets (A.S.). Even today, a multitude of ignorant and unimaginative people deny the truthfulness of the Holy Prophet (S.A.W.) due to bigotry and prejudice. It is now clear as daylight that the original Torah and Bible did contain references about the coming of the Holy Prophet (S.A.W.). It was for this reason that the rabbis, priests and bishops, who had read the original and unaltered Torah and Bible and who were really upright and honest and believed in Allah, openly confirmed the prophethood of the Holy Prophet (S.A.W.). It has been stated elsewhere in this book that the Holy Prophet (S.A.W.) had written a letter to the Pope at Rome and informed him about his prophethood. The Pope not only believed in his prophethood but also testified to it in a congregation. But the ignorant audience took it as an insult to their faith and in their wild fury beat the Pope to death. There are references to other Christian scholars, who also confirmed his Prophethood. But those who had a false sense of pride and were led astray by wordily considerations and lucre, not only kept the prophecies secret, but changed the scriptures. There were even penpictures of the Holy Prophet (S.A.W.) in the scriptures and these were intentionally changed so that the correct identity of the Holy Prophet (S.A.W.) might become dubious.

In the present day, expert artists can draw pictures of men, after carefully listening to the description about their physical features, particularly in respect of the eyes, nose, mouth, chin, hair, statue, build etc. Such imaginary pictures are usually fairly accurate. Similarly in ancient times, artists could draw pictures of men, after being appraised of their shape, size, stature, build and description of the face. In this book there is a reference to a letter which the Holy Prophet (S.A.W.) addressed to Caesar and entrusted it to the care of Dahiya (R.A.A.), who presented it to Caesar, at his court.

Ibne-Jauzi, a well known research worker and critic of Islamic history made an interesting revelation in the Biography of Umar (R.A.A.). He has disclosed that Dahiya (R.A.A). saw a large number of pictures on all sides of a room in the palace of Caesar. The latter informed him that they were the pictures of prophets and enquired of him, as to which was the picture of of the Holy Prophet (S.A.W.). After carefully looking at the picture, Dahiya pointed out to a picture and said that it was the picture of the Holy Prophet (S.A.W.). Caesar said, "Indeed! This is the picture of the Holy Prophet (S.A.W.). Again he enquired as to whose picture was to the right of it? Dahiya indicated that it was the picture of Abu Bakr Siddiq (R.A.A.), a companion of the Holy Prophet (S.A.W.). Then Caesar asked whose picture was to the left of it?" Dahiya stated that it was the picture of Umar Farooq (R.A.A.), the second companion." After listening to this Caesar said, "According to the prophesy of the Torah, these are the two persons, under whom your religion would attain its zenith".

Obviously some expert painter must have studied minutely the description of the Holy Prophet (S.A.W.) and his companions (R.A.A.) in the Torah and the Bible and then painted the pictures. This assumption is corroborated by the Holy Quran, which stated, "The people of the Book recognise (the Holy Prophet) just as they know their sons. But some of them (due to enmity and envy) intentionally suppress the truth". (Al -Quran, 2:17). Caesar stated that the pictures had come in his possession through the Prophet Danial. Jubair and Ibn-e-Wahab are also stated to have seen the pictures of the Holy Prophet (S.A.W.), in a Christian monastry at Basra and in the court of the Emperor of China, respectively.

There is another very important and interesting historical event which fully establishes beyond an iota of doubt that the people of the Book had certain and unambiguous evidence with the assistance of which they had little difficulty or hesitation in recognising the Holy prophet (S.A.W.) and his companions. It was the year 639 A.D. or 17th Hijri, 'Amr Bin Al-'Asa's laid siege to Jerusalem and sent a letter to the Commander of the place through a person who knew the Roman language, but he was instructed not to disclose that he knew the language. The idea was to ascertain the views of the people of Jerusalem. When the letter was read out, the commander said to his people that it seemed impossible that 'Amr Bin Al-'Aas would be in a position to capture Jerusalem, which could be conquered by a person in whose name there were three letters only. After this he described the man who would conquer Jerusalem and said that the description did not fit in with 'Amr. He, therefore, reached the conclusion that 'Amr would not be able to capture Jerusalem. In the circumstances he sent back the ambassador rather unconcernedly and unceremoniously. On his return he apprised 'Amr about all that he had heard. 'Amr said that the description corresponded with Umar Farooq (R.A.A.) who was caliph at that time.

When Umar (R.A.A.) was apprised of the position, he immediately went to Jerusalem, where he was immediately recognised by the people, who entrusted the city to him, without any hesitation. [1] This evidence about the truthfulness of the prophethood of Muhammad (S.A.W.) has reached mankind through Scriptures and history. But even otherwise it is not difficult to reach the same conclusion by logic or reason.

It is a fact that there have been real prophets and pseudo-prophets. But it does not seem to be difficult to differentiate between the two. It is true that it is the natural ambition of all men to reach the pinnacle of fame, become wealthy and wield influence, power and authority. To achieve these objectives, a man sometimes resorts to objectionable means. This is what brings in the difference. A true prophet is never attracted by these small temporal consideration and never deflects from the mission, for the attainment of which he is sent to this world.

When the Holy Prophet (S.A.W.), at the command of Allah, started bringing back the miscreants and transgressors on to the straight course and openly repudiated idol worship, the Quráish were shocked. They made fun of the Holy Prophet (S.A.W.), insulted and abused him and inflicted injuries and hurts on him. They thought that the Holy Prophet (S.A.W.) was actuated by a desire to gain fame, wealth, power and high status. Therefore Utba bin Rabia met the Holy Prophet (S.A.W.) on behalf of the Quraish and enquired of him as to what he desired? Did he want the State of Mecca? Or did he wish to marry a girl of a high family? Did he want a heap of wealth? They promised to place all those things at his disposal. They also agreed to place Mecca under his command, provided he refrained from his teachings. The Quraish were absolutely certain that he would accept their offer. In reply the Holy Prophet (S.A.W.) recited. Verses 6 to 9 of *Ha Meem Sajda* (Chapter of the Quran, which means:

---

1. *Tabari's History*, vol.4, p. 158, *Al-Bidaya wan Nihaya*, vol, 4, p. 55 and *Tarikh-ul-Kamil*, vol. 4, p.193.

"O! Muhammad. Say that I am a man like you. I have received a revelation that your God is Allah, the One. So go straight to him and ask for forgiveness from Him. Say, do you people deny Allah, who created this earth in two days. And you associate (others) with Allah. He is the Sustainer of the entire world."

When 'Utba returned, he was altogether a changed man. He informed the Quraish what Muhammad (S.A.W.) proffered was not poetry, but something else. He was, therefore, of the opinion that the Holy Prophet (S.A.W.) should not be interfered with. He further stated that If he is successful and takes ever Arabia it would be an honour for them; otherwise Arabia would put an end to him. The Quraish did not accept this course of action.

Umar (R.A.A.) was dead against Islam and the bitterest enemy of the Holy Prophet (S.A.W.). He was extremely agonstic towards even those who accepted Islam. At last he set out to put an end to the life of the Holy Prophet (S.A.W.). On the way, he incidentally met Naem Bin Abdullah, who enquired where he was going Umar (R.A.A.) informed him of his intentions. Naem told him first to set his own house in order and informed him that his sister and brother in-law had already embraced Islam. This further infuriated Umar (R.A.A.). He immediately returned and went to the house of his sister and heard them reciting the Holy Quran. They tried to hide the Quran, out of fear. He began to be labour his brother-in-law. His sister tried to save her husband, but Umar began to beat her too. But she said "Umar, do whatever you like Islam cannot be uprooted from my heart now." These words moved him much. He looked at his bleeding sister with compassion and love and asked her to recite what they were reading. His sister placed the Quran before him and he began to read, *Sura Al-Hadeed*, first verse of which is:

"Whatever is there in earth and heaven praises Allah. And Allah is All-powerful and All-wise."

He was highly impressed by each word. When he came to the beginning of verse 6 which says:

"Believe in Allah and His Prophet," he exclaimed, I testify that there is no god except Allah and that Muhammad is His Prophet." Immediately he hurried to the Holy Prophet (S.A.W.) who enquired, " Umar! with what intention have you come?" These words sent a shiver through him and he humbly answered, "To acquire belief (in Allah and His Prophet)."

This incident brought in a revolutionary change and Islam began to grow slowly. It was mainly due to the courage, fortitude, endurance, perseverance and patience of the Holy Prophet (S.A.W.) and his steadfast companions who cared little for hardships troubles, trials and tribulations, penury and privations. Even gold, silver and money was of little significance to them. Large quantities of gold, silver, dinars and dirhams were sent to the Holy Prophet (S.A.W.), but he distributed all of it to the needy, helpless and indigent. Once a piece of gold was left undisposed of. The Holy Prophet (S.A.W.) went home, but did not have peace of mind and could not rest until he had given the gold to a destitute. But in his own house no food could be cooked for days together. Here lies the real acid test of a person's truthfulness and above all, prophethood. Elsewhere in this book, there is a brief reference to a false prophet, who was after the worldly pelf, power and fame.

The Holy Prophet (S.A.W.) could have amassed countless wealth. He could have been a despotic and powerful emperor. He could have built for himself matchless palaces. He could have any number of servants and maids. But he would have none of these. He rather went penniless, ate coarse barley bread, which he gulped down his throat with the help of water, to satisfy his hunger. He would lie down on a bed of datepalm leaves or bare bedstead knitted with rough datepalm leaf strings, which left deep marks on his body. Once Umar (R.A.A.) went to see the Holy Prophet (S.A.W.) whom he found lying on a bedstead. There were deep marks on his body left by the rough strings. In a corner there was a handful of Oats. In another corner there hung a water skin. Tears ebbed into the eyes of Umar (R.A.A.) and he began to weep profusely. The Holy Prophet (S.A.W.) asked what made him weep. Umar (R.A.A.) said, "What a greater occasion could there be for weeping. Caesar and Kisra are rolling in the luxury of gardens and palaces and although you are a Prophet, so poor is your condition." The Holy Prophet (S.A.W.) calmly relied, "Are you not satisfied with the fact that they get this world and we the next one." Could there be a greater proof of his truthfulness.

The world cannot produce even a single example of any other person who shines so brilliantly in all the possible fields of human activity as does the Holy Prophet (S.A.W.). He was born an orphan and when he was 6 years old, his mother passed away. Thereafter he was brought up by his grandfather and after his death, by his uncle. At ten or twelve years of age, he tended goats. This was perhaps meant as an initiation into his future gigantic responsibility of guiding the entire world. he was taken by his uncle on a trade trip to Syria at the age of twelve. In Basra they alighted in a monastery of a Christian recluse, who on seeing the Holy Prophet (S.A.W.) said, "He is Syed-ul-Mursaleen" (Leader of the Prophets).

Thereafter the Holy Prophet (S.A.W.) as a child accompanied his uncle Abu Talib in his trade journeys many times and gained experience of trade deals. His fame as a man of fair, just and honest deals spread far and wide. Traders requested for his participation in their business enterprises which he gladly accepted. Thus we see him in his youth in the garb of an "Honest Trader". He presented himself as an epitome of truth, justice and uprightness. He would always stick to his word and promise and kept his dealings clean and above-board. People gave him the title of "Ameen" (Honest and truthful). It was on account of these qualities that Khadeeja (R.A.A.) a very wealthy and pious widow, requested him to take her trade goods to Syria and promised to pay him double the recompense, she usually paid to others. The Holy Prophet (S.A.W.) accepted the offer and took the goods to Syria Khadeeja (R.A.A.) sent the proposal of marriage to the Holy Prophet (S.A.W.) three months after his return and the marriage took place at her house.

After this comes the phase of prophethood. It must be stated in this connection that even before his prophethood the Holy Prophet (S.A.W.) always abstained from the customs which smacked of *shirk* (associating someone with Allah). He never paid any respect to any idol. He would often go to the cave of *Hira* and would stay there for days. There he would meditate and contemplate. It was there that he received the first revelation. The Holy Prophet (S.A.W.) got alarmed. When he came back and mentioned the matter to Khadeeja (R.A.A.), she took him to a Christian relative of her, Warqa Bin Naufil, who was a scholar of Torah and Bible. On hearing the whole event, he testified to his prophethood. He was not only a Prophet, but also a judge, a lawgiver, an administrator, a ruler, and a general too.

Whatever the capacity, in which he worked and however difficult the task before him, he proved to the world that he was the most judicious, just and equitable judge, for whom both friends and foes were equal; the noblest law giver and constitutionalist, most efficient and clearheaded administrator, and the most benign, gracious and benevolent ruler, who was more a benefactor, teacher and a servant of Allah than a ruler. As a general he was well aware of the strategy of war and even small details did not escape his notice. He would himself arrange the rank and file of the warriors and kept them in a straight line. He strictly prohibited hues and cries during the course of fighting. He himself gave instructions about all matters. In the battle of *Uhud*, the Muslims suffered heavily for not following his instructions.

In the 5th Hijri, the Quraish invaded Madina with a huge force of 24 thousand which comprised all the tribes of Arabia and Jews. The Holy Prophet (S.A.W.) saw that on three sides of Madina there were houses and datepalm gardens; which provided a good protection. He, therefore, had a ditch dug on the fourth unprotected side. The Quraish attacked with full force and fury. They could not, however, cross the ditch. As the battle continued for about a month, the enemy began to lose heart. At that time a strong wind uprooted the enemy tents. The enemy left the battle field absolutely disheartened.

Thus the Holy Prophet (S.A.W.) gave the proof of his perfection in all fields of life. The world has not thus far produced such a perfect personality.

Thus Allah is One and Omnipotent. All the Prophets (A.S.) particularly His last Prophet (S.A.W.), and His Books are true. Why should not all follow the right path of Allah, which alone leads to peace, tranquility, welfare and wellbeing of the entire mankind. Every human being, whatever his colour or language or country, deserves respect and has a right to live in this world with honour and in peace. It is now for us to make this world a heaven of peace or turn it into hell.

